# Reading Schedule 1

『이상한 나라의 앨리스』는 총 13,993개의 단어로 구성되어 있습니다.(중복 포함, 1페이지는 대략 172단어) 분당 150단어 읽기는 원어민이 말하는 속도입니다. 먼저 이 기준을 목표로 시작해보세요.

● 1회 읽기

| 날 짜 | / | / | / | / | / |
|---|---|---|---|---|---|
| 시 간 | ~ | ~ | ~ | ~ | ~ |
| 페이지 | ~ | ~ | ~ | ~ | ~ |

내용 이해도  ☑ 90%이상  ☑ 70%  ☑ 50%  ☑ 30%이하

리딩속도 계산   81  ÷  ☐  X  172  =  ☐
               전체 페이지   시간(분)   1페이지 당 평균 단어수   1분당 읽은 단어수

● 2회 읽기

| 날 짜 | / | / | / | / | / |
|---|---|---|---|---|---|
| 시 간 | ~ | ~ | ~ | ~ | ~ |
| 페이지 | ~ | ~ | ~ | ~ | ~ |

내용 이해도  ☑ 90%이상  ☑ 70%  ☑ 50%  ☑ 30%이하

리딩속도 계산   81  ÷  ☐  X  172  =  ☐
               전체 페이지   시간(분)   1페이지 당 평균 단어수   1분당 읽은 단어수

● 3회 읽기

| 날 짜 | / | / | / | / | / |
|---|---|---|---|---|---|
| 시 간 | ~ | ~ | ~ | ~ | ~ |
| 페이지 | ~ | ~ | ~ | ~ | ~ |

내용 이해도  ☑ 90%이상  ☑ 70%  ☑ 50%  ☑ 30%이하

리딩속도 계산   81  ÷  ☐  X  172  =  ☐
               전체 페이지   시간(분)   1페이지 당 평균 단어수   1분당 읽은 단어수

식은 죽 먹기야~

- 전체 평가

  체감 난이도　☑ 상　☑ 상중　☑ 중　☑ 중하　☑ 하

  읽기 만족도　☑ 나는 리딩의 고수!

  　　　　　　☑ 좀 잘했군요~

  　　　　　　☑ 노력하세요.

  　　　　　　☑ 난 머리가 안 좋나봐 -.-;

# Reading Schedule 2

『거울나라의 앨리스』 총 29,284개의 단어로 구성되어 있습니다.(중복 포함, 1페이지는 대략 171단어) 분당 150단어 읽기는 원어민이 말하는 속도입니다. 먼저 이 기준을 목표로 시작해보세요.

## ● 1회 읽기

| 날 짜 | / | / | / | / | / |
|---|---|---|---|---|---|
| 시 간 | ~ | ~ | ~ | ~ | ~ |
| 페이지 | ~ | ~ | ~ | ~ | ~ |

내용 이해도 ✓ 90%이상 ✓ 70% ✓ 50% ✓ 30%이하

리딩속도 계산 | 171 | ÷ | | X | 171 | = | |
전체 페이지 / 시간(분) / 1페이지 당 평균 단어수 / 1분당 읽은 단어수

## ● 2회 읽기

| 날 짜 | / | / | / | / | / |
|---|---|---|---|---|---|
| 시 간 | ~ | ~ | ~ | ~ | ~ |
| 페이지 | ~ | ~ | ~ | ~ | ~ |

내용 이해도 ✓ 90%이상 ✓ 70% ✓ 50% ✓ 30%이하

리딩속도 계산 | 171 | ÷ | | X | 171 | = | |
전체 페이지 / 시간(분) / 1페이지 당 평균 단어수 / 1분당 읽은 단어수

## ● 3회 읽기

| 날 짜 | / | / | / | / | / |
|---|---|---|---|---|---|
| 시 간 | ~ | ~ | ~ | ~ | ~ |
| 페이지 | ~ | ~ | ~ | ~ | ~ |

내용 이해도 ✓ 90%이상 ✓ 70% ✓ 50% ✓ 30%이하

리딩속도 계산 | 171 | ÷ | | X | 171 | = | |
전체 페이지 / 시간(분) / 1페이지 당 평균 단어수 / 1분당 읽은 단어수

식은 죽
먹기야~

- 전체 평가

  체감 난이도  ☑ 상  ☑ 상중  ☑ 중  ☑ 중하  ☑ 하

  읽기 만족도  ☑ 나는 리딩의 고수!
  ☑ 좀 잘했군요~
  ☑ 노력하세요.
  ☑ 난 머리가 안 좋나봐 -.-;

이상한 나라의 앨리스
+
거울 나라의 앨리스

리딩 속도가 빨라지는 영어책 006

## 이상한 나라의 앨리스 + 거울 나라의 앨리스
Alice's Adventures in Wonderland
Through The Looking-Rrass

2015년 5월 20일 초판 1쇄 인쇄
2015년 5월 25일 초판 1쇄 발행

**지은이** 루이스 캐럴
**발행인** 손건
**편집기획** 김상배
**마케팅** 이언영
**디자인** 김선옥
**제작** 최승용
**인쇄** 선경프린테크

**발행처 LanCom 랭컴**
**주소** 서울시 영등포구 영신로 38길 17
**등록번호** 제 312-2006-00060호
**전화** 02) 2636-0895
**팩스** 02) 2636-0896
**홈페이지** www.lancom.co.kr

ISBN 978-89-98469-77-1

# 이상한 나라의 앨리스

## Alice's Adventures in Wonderland

루이스 캐럴 지음

## ✥ 『이상한 나라의 앨리스』 줄거리

**1장:** 강둑에 앉아 있던 앨리스는 사람처럼 옷을 입고 회중시계를 보면서 바쁘게 뛰어가는 토끼를 발견하고 토끼를 따라 굴 속으로 들어간다. 앨리스는 탁자 위에 있는 병을 마시고 몸이 작아진다.

**2장:** 탁자 밑에서 발견한 케이크를 먹자 몸이 커져서 옴짝달싹 못하게 된 앨리스가 울자 눈물 웅덩이가 생겼다. 그 때 다시 토끼를 발견하고 앨리스가 소리쳐 부르자 토끼는 놀라 부채와 장갑을 떨어뜨리고 달아난다. 앨리스가 부채를 주워 부치자 몸이 다시 작아졌고, 앨리스는 눈물 웅덩이에 빠진다.

**3장:** 앨리스는 눈물 웅덩이에 빠져 있던 다른 동물들과 함께 헤엄쳐서 둑으로 올라온다. 몸을 말리며 이런 저런 이야기를 나누던 중, 앨리스가 애완 고양이 이야기를 꺼내자 다들 겁을 먹고 뿔뿔이 흩어진다.

**4장:** 혼자 남은 앨리스에게 장갑과 부채를 잃어버린 토끼가 찾아온다. 토끼는 앨리스를 하녀로 착각해 심부름을 보내고, 앨리스는 그 곳에서 또 다른 병을 발견한다. 그 병을 마시자 앨리스의 몸이 커졌다. 토끼가 창문으로 쏟아부은 케이크를 먹고 앨리스는 다시 작아진다.

**5장:** 애벌레를 만난 앨리스는 몸이 커지는 버섯과 작아지는 버섯을 알게 되고, 원하는 키를 맞춘다.

**6장:** 제복을 입은 물고기를 만난 앨리스는 공작 부인의 집을 방문한다. 공작 부인이 맡긴 아기가 돼지로 변해버리자 앨리스는 돼지를 숲에 풀어주고, 몸이 사라졌다 나타났다 하는 고양이를 만나 이야기를 나눈다.

**7장:** 앨리스는 삼월 토끼와 모자 장수가 차를 마시고 있는 다과회에 간다.

**8장:** 앨리스는 플라밍고로 고슴도치를 치는 이상한 크로켓 경기에 참가한다. 하트 여왕은 보는 사람마다 트집을 잡으며 목을 치라고 명령한다.

9장: 하트 여왕은 앨리스에게 그리폰을 타고 모조 거북을 만나고 오라고 명령한다.

**10장:** 모조 거북은 한숨을 쉬며 바다가재 카드리유에 대한 이야기를 들려준다. 멀리서 재판이 시작되었다는 외침이 들리자, 그리폰은 앨리스를 데리고 되돌아간다.

**11장:** 하트 여왕의 타르트를 훔친 잭에 대한 재판이 시작되고 증인들이 차례대로 심문을 받지만, 결정적인 증거를 제시하지 못한다. 앨리스는 커다랗게 변해서 이 자리를 빠져 나가는 게 좋겠다는 이상한 느낌이 들었다.

**12장:** 버섯을 먹고 몸이 커진 앨리스는 마지막 증인으로 호출된다. 여왕은 증거도 없이 잭을 처형하려 하지만, 앨리스가 반대한다. 그러자 카드들이 모두 일어서 앨리스에게 떨어져 내렸다. 앨리스가 비명을 지르며 카드를 떨쳐내려 하는 순간 잠에서 깨어난다.

# CONTENTS

## CHAPTER I
Down the Rabbit-Hole

*12*

## CHAPTER II
The Pool of Tears

*19*

## CHAPTER III
A Caucus-Race and a Long Tale

*25*

## CHAPTER IV
The Rabbit Sends in a Little Bill

*33*

## CHAPTER V
Advice from a Caterpillar

*40*

## CHAPTER VI
Pig and Pepper

*46*

**CHAPTER VII**

A Mad Tea-Party

*52*

**CHAPTER VIII**

The Queen's Croquet-Ground

*56*

**CHAPTER IX**

The Mock Turtle's Story

*63*

**CHAPTER X**

The Lobster Quadrille

*77*

**CHAPTER XI**

Who Stole the Tarts?

*91*

**CHAPTER XII**

Alice's Evidence

*95*

# CHAPTER I
# Down the Rabbit-Hole

Alice was beginning to get very tired of sitting by her sister on the bank, and of having nothing to do. Once or twice she had peeped into the book her sister was reading, but it had no pictures or conversations in it, "and what is the use of a book," thought Alice, "without pictures or conversations?"

So she was considering in her own mind (as well as she could, for the day made her feel very sleepy and stupid), whether the pleasure of making a daisy-chain would be worth the trouble of getting up and picking the daisies, when suddenly a White Rabbit with pink eyes ran close by her.

There was nothing so very remarkable in that, nor did Alice think it so very much out of the way to hear the Rabbit say to itself, "Oh dear! Oh dear! I shall be too late!" But when the Rabbit actually took a watch out of its waistcoat-pocket and looked at it and then hurried on, Alice started to her feet, for it flashed across her mind that she had never before seen a rabbit with either a waistcoat-pocket, or a watch to take out of it, and, burning with curiosity, she ran across the field after it and was just in time to see it pop down a large rabbit-hole, under the hedge. In another moment, down went Alice after it!

The rabbit-hole went straight on like a tunnel for some way and then dipped suddenly down, so suddenly that Alice had not a moment to think about stopping herself before she found herself falling down what seemed to be a very deep well.

Either the well was very deep, or she fell very slowly, for she had plenty of time, as she went down, to look about her. First, she tried to make out what she was coming to, but it was too dark to see anything; then she looked at the sides of the well and noticed that they were filled with cupboards and book-shelves; here and there she saw maps and pictures hung upon pegs. She took down a jar from one of the shelves as she passed. It was labeled "ORANGE MARMALADE," but, to her great disappointment, it was empty; she did not like to drop the jar, so managed to put it into one of the cupboards as she fell past it.

Down, down, down! Would the fall never come to an end? There was nothing else to do, so Alice soon began talking to herself. "Dinah'll miss me very much to-night, I should think!" (Dinah was the cat.) "I hope they'll remember her saucer of milk at tea-time. Dinah, my dear, I wish you were down here with me!" Alice felt that she was dozing off, when suddenly, thump! thump! down she came upon a heap of sticks and dry leaves, and the fall was over.

Alice was not a bit hurt, and she jumped up in a moment. She looked up, but it was all dark overhead; before her was another long passage and the White Rabbit was still in sight, hurrying down it. There was not a moment to be lost. Away went Alice like the wind and was just in time to hear it say, as it turned a corner, "Oh, my ears and whiskers, how late it's getting!" She was close behind it when she turned the corner, but the Rabbit was no longer to be seen.

She found herself in a long, low hall, which

was lit up by a row of lamps hanging from the roof. There were doors all round the hall, but they were all locked; and when Alice had been all the way down one side and up the other, trying every door, she walked sadly down the middle, wondering how she was ever to get out again.

Suddenly she came upon a little table, all made of solid glass. There was nothing on it but a tiny golden key, and Alice's first idea was that this might belong to one of the doors of the hall; but, alas! either the locks were too large, or the key was too small, but, at any rate, it would not open any of them. However, on the second time round, she came upon a low curtain she had not noticed before, and behind it was a little door about fifteen inches high. She tried the little golden key in the lock, and to her great delight, it fitted!

Alice opened the door and found that it led into a small passage, not much larger than a rat-hole; she knelt down and looked along the passage into the loveliest garden you ever saw. How she longed to get out of that dark hall and wander about among those beds of bright flowers and those cool fountains, but she could not even get her head through the doorway. "Oh," said Alice, "how I wish I could shut up like a telescope! I think I could, if I only knew how to begin."

Alice went back to the table, half hoping she might find another key on it, or at any rate, a book of rules for shutting people up like telescopes. This time she found a little bottle on it ("which certainly was not here before," said Alice), and tied round the neck of the bottle was a paper label, with the words "DRINK ME" beautifully printed on it in large letters.

"No, I'll look first," she said, "and see whether it's marked '*poison*' or not," for she had never forgotten that, if you drink from a bottle marked "poison," it is almost certain to disagree with you, sooner or later. However, this bottle was *not* marked "poison," so Alice ventured to taste it, and, finding it very nice (it had a sort of mixed flavor of cherry-tart, custard, pineapple, roast turkey, toffy and hot buttered toast), she very soon finished it off.

\* \* \* \* \*

"What a curious feeling!" said Alice. "I must be shutting up like a telescope!"

And so it was indeed! She was now only ten inches high, and her face brightened up at the thought that she was now the right size for going through the little door into that lovely garden.

After awhile, finding that nothing more happened, she decided on going into the garden at once; but, alas for poor Alice! When she got to the door, she found she had forgotten the little golden key, and when she went back to the table for it, she found she could not possibly reach it: she could see it quite plainly through the glass and she tried her best to climb up one of the legs of the table, but it was too slippery, and when she had tired herself out with trying, the poor little thing sat down and cried.

"Come, there's no use in crying like that!" said Alice to herself rather sharply. "I advise you to leave off this minute!" She generally gave herself very good advice (though she very seldom followed it), and sometimes she scolded herself so severely as to bring tears into her eyes.

Soon her eye fell on a little glass box that was lying under the table: she opened it and found in it a very small cake, on which the words "EAT ME" were beautifully marked in currants. "Well, I'll eat it," said Alice, "and if it makes me grow larger, I can reach the key; and if it makes me grow smaller, I can creep under the door: so either way I'll get into the garden, and I don't care which happens!"

She ate a little bit and said anxiously to herself, "Which way? Which way?" holding her hand on the top of her head to feel which way she was growing; and she was quite surprised to find that she remained the same size. So she set to work and very soon finished off the cake.

# CHAPTER II
# The Pool of Tears

"Curiouser and curiouser!" cried Alice (she was so much surprised that for the moment she quite forgot how to speak good English). "Now I'm opening out like the largest telescope that ever was! Good-by, feet! Oh, my poor little feet, I wonder who will put on your shoes and stockings for you now, dears? I shall be a great deal too far off to trouble myself about you."

Just at this moment her head struck against the roof of the hall; in fact, she was now rather more than nine feet high, and she at once took up the little golden key and hurried off to the garden door.

Poor Alice! It was as much as she could do, lying down on one side, to look through into the garden with one eye; but to get through was more hopeless than ever. She sat down and began to cry again.

She went on shedding gallons of tears, until

there was a large pool all round her and reaching half down the hall.

After a time, she heard a little pattering of feet in the distance and she hastily dried her eyes to see what was coming. It was the White Rabbit returning, s'plendidly dressed, with a pair of white kid-gloves in one hand and a large fan in the other. He came trotting along in a great hurry, muttering to himself, "Oh! the Duchess, the Duchess! Oh! *won't* she be savage if I've kept her waiting!"

When the Rabbit came near her, Alice began, in a low, timid voice, "If you please, sir—" The Rabbit started violently, dropped the white kid-gloves and the fan and skurried away into the darkness as hard as he could go.

Alice took up the fan and gloves and she kept fanning herself all the time she went on talking. "Dear, dear! How queer everything is to-day! And yesterday things went on just as usual. *Was* I the same when I got up this morning? But if I'm not the same, the next question is, 'Who in the world am I?' Ah, *that's* the great puzzle!"

As she said this, she looked down at her hands

and was surprised to see that she had put on one of the Rabbit's little white kid-gloves while she was talking. "How *can* I have done that?" she thought. "I must be growing small again." She got up and went to the table to measure herself by it and found that she was now about two feet high and was going on shrinking rapidly. She soon found out that the cause of this was the fan she was holding and she dropped it hastily, just in time to save herself from shrinking away altogether.

"That *was* a narrow escape!" said Alice, a good deal frightened at the sudden change, but very glad to find herself still in existence. "And now for the garden!" And she ran with all speed back to the little door; but, alas! the little door was shut again and the little golden key was lying on the glass table as before. "Things are worse than ever," thought the poor child, "for I never was so small as this before, never!"

As she said these words, her foot slipped, and in another moment, splash! she was up to her chin in salt-water. Her first idea was that she had somehow fallen into the sea. However, she soon made out that she was in the pool of tears which she had wept when she was nine feet high.

Just then she heard something splashing about in the pool a little way off, and she swam nearer to see what it was: she soon made out that it was only a mouse that had slipped in like herself.

"Would it be of any use, now," thought Alice, "to speak to this mouse? Everything is so out-of-the-way down here that I should think very likely it can talk; at any rate, there's no harm in trying." So she began, "O Mouse, do you know the way out of this pool? I am very tired of swimming about here, O Mouse!" The Mouse looked at her rather inquisitively and seemed to her to wink with one of its little eyes, but it said nothing.

"Perhaps it doesn't understand English," thought Alice. "I dare say it's a French mouse, come over with William the Conqueror." So she began again: "Où est ma chatte?" which was the first sentence in her French lesson-book. The Mouse gave a sudden leap out of the water and seemed to quiver all over with fright. "Oh, I beg your pardon!" cried Alice hastily, afraid that she had hurt the poor animal's feelings. "I quite forgot you didn't like cats."

"Not like cats!" cried the Mouse in a shrill, passionate voice. "Would *you* like cats, if you were me?"

"Well, perhaps not," said Alice in a soothing tone; "don't be angry about it. And yet I wish I could show you our cat Dinah. I think you'd take a fancy to cats, if you could only see her. She is such a dear, quiet thing." The Mouse was bristling all over and she felt certain it must be really offended. "We won't talk about her any more, if you'd rather not."

"We, indeed!" cried the Mouse, who was trembling down to the end of its tail. "As if *I* would talk on such a subject! Our family always *hated* cats—nasty, low, vulgar things! Don't let me hear the name again!"

"I won't indeed!" said Alice, in a great hurry to change the subject of conversation. "Are you-are you fond—of—of dogs? There is such a nice little dog near our house, I should like to show you! It kills all the rats and—oh, dear!" cried Alice in a sorrowful tone. "I'm afraid I've offended it again!" For the Mouse was swimming away from her as hard as it could go, and making quite a commotion in the pool as it went.

So she called softly after it, "Mouse dear! Do come back again, and we won't talk about cats, or dogs either, if you don't like them!" When the Mouse heard this, it turned round and swam slowly back to her; its face was quite pale, and it said, in a low, trembling voice, "Let us get to the shore and then I'll tell you my history and you'll understand why it is I hate cats and dogs."

It was high time to go, for the pool was getting quite crowded with the birds and animals that had fallen into it; there were a Duck and a Dodo, a Lory and an Eaglet, and several other curious creatures. Alice led the way and the whole party swam to the shore.

# CHAPTER III

## A Caucus-Race and a Long Tale

They were indeed a queer-looking party that assembled on the bank—the birds with draggled feathers, the animals with their fur clinging close to them, and all dripping wet, cross and uncomfortable.

The first question, of course, was how to get dry again. They had a consultation about this and after a few minutes, it seemed quite natural to Alice to find herself talking familiarly with them, as if she had known them all her life.

At last the Mouse, who seemed to be a person of some authority among them, called out, "Sit down, all of you, and listen to me! *I'll* soon make you dry enough!" They all sat down at once, in a large ring, with the Mouse in the middle.

"Ahem!" said the Mouse with an important air. "Are you all ready? This is the driest thing I know. Silence all round, if you please! 'William the Conqueror, whose cause was favored by the pope, was soon submitted to by the English, who wanted leaders, and had been of late much accustomed to usurpation and conquest. Edwin and Morcar, the Earls of Mercia and Northumbria'—"

"Ugh!" said the Lory, with a shiver.

"—'And even Stigand, the patriotic archbishop of Canterbury, found it advisable'—"

"Found *what*?" said the Duck.

"Found *it*," the Mouse replied rather crossly; "of course, you know what 'It' means."

"I know what 'It' means well enough, when *I* find a thing," said the Duck; "it's generally a frog or a worm. The question is, what did the archbishop find?"

The Mouse did not notice this question, but hurriedly went on, "'—found it advisable to go with Edgar Atheling to meet William and offer him the crown.'—How are you getting on now, my dear?" it continued, turning to Alice as it spoke.

"As wet as ever," said Alice in a melancholy tone; "it doesn't seem to dry me at all."

"In that case," said the Dodo solemnly, rising to its feet, "I move that the meeting adjourn, for the immediate adoption of more energetic remedies—"

"Speak English!" said the Eaglet. "I don't know the meaning of half those long words, and, what's more, I don't believe you do either!"

"What I was going to say," said the Dodo in an offended tone, "is that the best thing to get us dry would be a Caucus-race."

"What *is* a Caucus-race?" said Alice.

"Why," said the Dodo, "the best way to explain it is to do it." First it marked out a race-course, in a sort of circle, and then all the party were placed along the course, here and there. There was no "One, two, three and away!" but they began running when they liked and left off when they liked, so that it was not easy to know when the race was over. However, when they had been running half an hour or so and were quite dry again, the Dodo suddenly called out, "The race is over!" and they all crowded round it, panting and asking, "But who has won?"

This question the Dodo could not answer without a great deal of thought. At last it said,

"*Everybody* has won, and *all* must have prizes."

"But who is to give the prizes?" quite a chorus of voices asked.

"Why, *she*, of course," said the Dodo, pointing to Alice with one finger; and the whole party at once crowded round her, calling out, in a confused way, "Prizes! Prizes!"

Alice had no idea what to do, and in despair she put her hand into her pocket and pulled out a box of comfits (luckily the salt-water had not got into it) and handed them round as prizes. There was exactly one a-piece, all round.

The next thing was to eat the comfits; this caused some noise and confusion, as the large birds complained that they could not taste theirs, and the small ones choked and had to be patted on the back. However, it was over at last and they sat down again in a ring and begged the Mouse to tell them something more.

"You promised to tell me your history, you know," said Alice, "and why it is you hate—C and D," she added in a whisper, half afraid that it would be offended again.

"Mine is a long and a sad tale!" said the Mouse, turning to Alice and sighing.

"It *is* a long tail, certainly," said Alice, looking down with wonder at the Mouse's tail, "but why do you call it sad?" And she kept on puzzling about it while the Mouse was speaking, so that her idea of the tale was something like this:—

"Fury said to

a mouse, That

he met in the

house, 'Let

us both go

to law: *I*

will prosecute

*you.*—

Come, I'll

take no denial:

We must have

the trial;

For really

this morning

I've

nothing to do.' Said the mouse to the cur, 'Such a trial, dear sir, With no jury or judge, would be wasting our breath.' 'I'll be judge, I'll be jury,' said cunning old Fury; 'I'll try

the

whole

cause,

and

condemn

you to

death.'"


"You are not attending!" said the Mouse to Alice, severely. "What are you thinking of?"

"I beg your pardon," said Alice very humbly, "you had got to the fifth bend, I think?"

"You insult me by talking such nonsense!" said the Mouse, getting up and walking away.

"Please come back and finish your story!" Alice called after it. And the others all joined in chorus, "Yes, please do!" But the Mouse only shook its head impatiently and walked a little quicker.

"I wish I had Dinah, our cat, here!" said Alice. This caused a remarkable sensation among the party. Some of the birds hurried off at once, and a Canary called out in a trembling voice, to its children, "Come away, my dears! It's high time you were all in bed!" On various pretexts they all moved off and Alice was soon left alone.

"I wish I hadn't mentioned Dinah! Nobody seems to like her down here and I'm sure she's the best cat in the world!" Poor Alice began to cry again, for she felt very lonely and low-spirited. In a little while, however, she again heard a little pattering of footsteps in the distance and she looked up eagerly.

# CHAPTER IV
# The Rabbit Sends in a Little Bill

It was the White Rabbit, trotting slowly back again and looking anxiously about as it went, as if it had lost something; Alice heard it muttering to itself, "The Duchess! The Duchess! Oh, my dear paws! Oh, my fur and whiskers! She'll get me executed, as sure as ferrets are ferrets! Where *can* I have dropped them, I wonder?" Alice guessed in a moment that it was looking for the fan and the pair of white kid-gloves and she very good-naturedly began hunting about for them, but they were nowhere to be seen—everything seemed to have changed since her swim in the pool, and the great hall, with the glass table and the little door, had vanished completely.

Very soon the Rabbit noticed Alice, and called to her, in an angry tone, "Why, Mary Ann, what *are* you doing out here? Run home this moment and fetch me a pair of gloves and a fan! Quick, now!"

"He took me for his housemaid!" said Alice, as she ran off. "How surprised he'll be when he finds out who I am!" As she said this, she came upon a neat little house, on the door of which was a bright brass plate with the name "W. RABBIT" engraved upon it. She went in without knocking and hurried upstairs, in great fear lest she should meet the real Mary Ann and be turned out of the house before she had found the fan and gloves.

By this time, Alice had found her way into a tidy little room with a table in the window, and on it a fan and two or three pairs of tiny white kid-gloves; she took up the fan and a pair of the gloves and was just going to leave the room, when her eyes fell upon a little bottle that stood near the looking-glass. She uncorked it and put it to her lips, saying to herself, "I do hope it'll make me grow large again, for, really, I'm quite tired of being such a tiny little thing!"

Before she had drunk half the bottle, she found her head pressing against the ceiling, and had to stoop to save her neck from being broken. She hastily put down the bottle, remarking, "That's quite enough—I hope I sha'n't grow any more."

Alas! It was too late to wish that! She went on growing and growing and very soon she had to kneel down on the floor. Still she went on growing, and, as a last resource, she put one arm out of the window and one foot up the chimney, and said to herself, "Now I can do no more, whatever happens. What *will* become of me?"

Luckily for Alice, the little magic bottle had now had its full effect and she grew no larger. After a few minutes she heard a voice outside and stopped to listen.

"Mary Ann! Mary Ann!" said the voice. "Fetch me my gloves this moment!" Then came a little pattering of feet on the stairs. Alice knew it was the Rabbit coming to look for her and she trembled till she shook the house, quite forgetting that she was now about a thousand times as large as the Rabbit and had no reason to be afraid of it.

Presently the Rabbit came up to the door and tried to open it; but as the door opened inwards and Alice's elbow was pressed hard against it, that attempt proved a failure. Alice heard it say to itself, "Then I'll go round and get in at the window."

"*That* you won't!" thought Alice; and after waiting till she fancied she heard the Rabbit just under the window, she suddenly spread out her hand and made a snatch in the air. She did not get hold of anything, but she heard a little shriek and a fall and a crash of broken glass, from which she concluded that it was just possible it had fallen into a cucumber-frame or something of that sort.

Next came an angry voice—the Rabbit's—"Pat! Pat! Where are you?" And then a voice she had never heard before, "Sure then, I'm here! Digging for apples, yer honor!"

"Here! Come and help me out of this! Now tell me, Pat, what's that in the window?"

"Sure, it's an arm, yer honor!"

"Well, it's got no business there, at any rate; go and take it away!"

There was a long silence after this and Alice could only hear whispers now and then, and at last she spread out her hand again and made another snatch in the air. This time there were *two* little shrieks and more sounds of broken glass. "I wonder what they'll do next!" thought Alice. "As for pulling me out of the window, I only wish they *could*!"

She waited for some time without hearing anything more. At last came a rumbling of little cart-wheels and the sound of a good many voices all talking together. She made out the words: "Where's the other ladder? Bill's got the other-Bill! Here, Bill! Will the roof bear?—Who's to go down the chimney?—Nay, *I* sha'n't! *you* do it! Here, Bill! The master says you've got to go down the chimney!"

Alice drew her foot as far down the chimney as she could and waited till she heard a little animal scratching and scrambling about in the chimney close above her; then she gave one sharp kick and waited to see what would happen next.

The first thing she heard was a general chorus of "There goes Bill!" then the Rabbit's voice alone—"Catch him, you by the hedge!" Then silence and then another confusion of voices-"Hold up his head—Brandy now—Don't choke him—What happened to you?"

Last came a little feeble, squeaking voice, "Well, I hardly know—No more, thank ye. I'm better now—all I know is, something comes at me like a Jack-in-the-box and up I goes like a sky-rocket!"

After a minute or two of silence, they began moving about again, and Alice heard the Rabbit say, "A barrowful will do, to begin with."

"A barrowful of *what*?" thought Alice. But she had not long to doubt, for the next moment a shower of little pebbles came rattling in at the window and some of them hit her in the face. Alice noticed, with some surprise, that the pebbles were all turning into little cakes as they lay on the floor and a bright idea came into her head. "If I eat one of these cakes," she thought, "it's sure to make *some* change in my size."

So she swallowed one of the cakes and was delighted to find that she began shrinking directly. As soon as she was small enough to get through the door, she ran out of the house and found quite a crowd of little animals and birds waiting outside. They all made a rush at Alice the moment she appeared, but she ran off as hard as she could and soon found herself safe in a thick wood.

"The first thing I've got to do," said Alice to herself, as she wandered about in the wood, "is to grow to my right size again; and the second thing is to find my way into that lovely garden. I suppose I ought to eat or drink something or other, but the great question is 'What?'"

Alice looked all around her at the flowers and the blades of grass, but she could not see anything that looked like the right thing to eat or drink under the circumstances. There was a large mushroom growing near her, about the same height as herself. She stretched herself up on tiptoe and peeped over the edge and her eyes immediately met those of a large blue caterpillar, that was sitting on the top, with its arms folded, quietly smoking a long hookah and taking not the smallest notice of her or of anything else.

# CHAPTER V

## Advice from a Caterpillar

At last the Caterpillar took the hookah out of its mouth and addressed Alice in a languid, sleepy voice.

"Who are *you*?" said the Caterpillar.

Alice replied, rather shyly, "I—I hardly know, sir, just at present—at least I know who I *was* when I got up this morning, but I think I must have changed several times since then."

"What do you mean by that?" said the Caterpillar, sternly. "Explain yourself!"

"I can't explain *myself*, I'm afraid, sir," said Alice, "because I'm not myself, you see—being so many different sizes in a day is very confusing." She drew herself up and said very gravely, "I think you ought to tell me who *you* are, first."

"Why?" said the Caterpillar.

As Alice could not think of any good reason and the Caterpillar seemed to be in a *very* unpleasant state of mind, she turned away.

"Come back!" the Caterpillar called after her. "I've something important to say!" Alice turned and came back again.

"Keep your temper," said the Caterpillar.

"Is that all?" said Alice, swallowing down her anger as well as she could.

"No," said the Caterpillar.

It unfolded its arms, took the hookah out of its mouth again, and said, "So you think you're changed, do you?"

"I'm afraid, I am, sir," said Alice. "I can't remember things as I used—and I don't keep the same size for ten minutes together!"

"What size do you want to be?" asked the Caterpillar.

"Oh, I'm not particular as to size," Alice hastily replied, "only one doesn't like changing so often, you know. I should like to be a *little* larger, sir, if you wouldn't mind," said Alice. "Three inches is such a wretched height to be."

"It is a very good height indeed!" said the Caterpillar angrily, rearing itself upright as it spoke (it was exactly three inches high).

In a minute or two, the Caterpillar got down off the mushroom and crawled away into the grass, merely remarking, as it went, "One side will make you grow taller, and the other side will make you grow shorter."

"One side of *what*? The other side of *what*?" thought Alice to herself.

"Of the mushroom," said the Caterpillar, just as if she had asked it aloud; and in another moment, it was out of sight.

Alice remained looking thoughtfully at the mushroom for a minute, trying to make out which were the two sides of it. At last she stretched her arms round it as far as they would go, and broke off a bit of the edge with each hand.

"And now which is which?" she said to herself, and nibbled a little of the right-hand bit to try the effect. The next moment she felt a violent blow underneath her chin—it had struck her foot!

She was a good deal frightened by this very sudden change, as she was shrinking rapidly; so she set to work at once to eat some of the other bit. Her chin was pressed so closely against her foot that there was hardly room to open her mouth; but she did it at last and managed to swallow a morsel of the left-hand bit....

"Come, my head's free at last!" said Alice; but all she could see, when she looked down, was an immense length of neck, which seemed to rise like a stalk out of a sea of green leaves that lay far below her.

"Where *have* my shoulders got to? And oh, my poor hands, how is it I can't see you?" She was delighted to find that her neck would bend about easily in any direction, like a serpent. She had just succeeded in curving it down into a graceful zigzag and was going to dive in among the leaves, when a sharp hiss made her draw back in a hurry—a large pigeon had flown into her face and was beating her violently with its wings.

"Serpent!" cried the Pigeon.

"I'm *not* a serpent!" said Alice indignantly. "Let me alone!"

"I've tried the roots of trees, and I've tried banks, and I've tried hedges," the Pigeon went on, "but those serpents! There's no pleasing them!"

Alice was more and more puzzled.

"As if it wasn't trouble enough hatching the eggs," said the Pigeon, "but I must be on the look-out for serpents, night and day! And just as I'd taken the highest tree in the wood," continued the Pigeon, raising its voice to a shriek, "and just as I was thinking I should be free of them at last, they must needs come wriggling down from the sky! Ugh, Serpent!"

"But I'm *not* a serpent, I tell you!" said Alice. "I'm a—I'm a—I'm a little girl," she added rather doubtfully, as she remembered the number of changes she had gone through that day.

"You're looking for eggs, I know *that* well enough," said the Pigeon; "and what does it matter to me whether you're a little girl or a serpent?"

"It matters a good deal to *me*," said Alice hastily; "but I'm not looking for eggs, as it happens, and if I was, I shouldn't want *yours*—I don't like them raw."

"Well, be off, then!" said the Pigeon in a sulky tone, as it settled down again into its nest. Alice crouched down among the trees as well as she could, for her neck kept getting entangled among the branches, and every now and then she had to stop and untwist it. After awhile she remembered that she still held the pieces of mushroom in her hands, and she set to work very carefully, nibbling first at one and then at the other, and growing sometimes taller and sometimes shorter, until she had succeeded in bringing herself down to her usual height.

It was so long since she had been anything near the right size that it felt quite strange at first. "The next thing is to get into that beautiful garden—how *is* that to be done, I wonder?" As she said this, she came suddenly upon an open place, with a little house in it about four feet high. "Whoever lives there," thought Alice, "it'll never do to come upon them *this* size; why, I should frighten them out of their wits!" She did not venture to go near the house till she had brought herself down to nine inches high.

# CHAPTER VI
## Pig and Pepper

For a minute or two she stood looking at the house, when suddenly a footman in livery came running out of the wood (judging by his face only, she would have called him a fish)—and rapped loudly at the door with his knuckles. It was opened by another footman in livery, with a round face and large eyes like a frog.

The Fish-Footman began by producing from under his arm a great letter, and this he handed over to the other, saying, in a solemn tone, "For the Duchess. An invitation from the Queen to play croquet." The Frog-Footman repeated, in the same solemn tone, "From the Queen. An invitation for the Duchess to play croquet." Then they both bowed low and their curls got entangled together.

When Alice next peeped out, the Fish-Footman was gone, and the other was sitting on the ground near the door, staring stupidly up into the sky. Alice went timidly up to the door and knocked.

"There's no sort of use in knocking," said the Footman, "and that for two reasons. First, because I'm on the same side of the door as you are; secondly, because they're making such a noise inside, no one could possibly hear you." And certainly there *was* a most extraordinary noise going on within—a constant howling and sneezing, and every now and then a great crash, as if a dish or kettle had been broken to pieces.

"How am I to get in?" asked Alice.

"*are* you to get in at all?" said the Footman. "That's the first question, you know."

Alice opened the door and went in. The door led right into a large kitchen, which was full of smoke from one end to the other; the Duchess was sitting on a three-legged stool in the middle, nursing a baby; the cook was leaning over the fire, stirring a large caldron which seemed to be full of soup.

"There's certainly too much pepper in that soup!" Alice said to herself, as well as she could for sneezing. Even the Duchess sneezed occasionally; and as for the baby, it was sneezing and howling alternately without a moment's pause. The only two creatures in the kitchen that did *not* sneeze were the cook and a large cat, which was grinning from ear to ear.

"Please would you tell me," said Alice, a little timidly, "why your cat grins like that?"

"It's a Cheshire-Cat," said the Duchess, "and that's why."

"I didn't know that Cheshire-Cats always grinned; in fact, I didn't know that cats *could* grin," said Alice.

"You don't know much," said the Duchess, "and that's a fact."

Just then the cook took the caldron of soup off the fire, and at once set to work throwing everything within her reach at the Duchess and the baby—the fire-irons came first; then followed a shower of saucepans, plates and dishes. The Duchess took no notice of them, even when they hit her, and the baby was howling so much already that it was quite impossible to say whether the blows hurt it or not.

"Oh, *please* mind what you're doing!" cried Alice, jumping up and down in an agony of terror.

"Here! You may nurse it a bit, if you like!" the Duchess said to Alice, flinging the baby at her as she spoke. "I must go and get ready to play croquet with the Queen," and she hurried out of the room.

Alice caught the baby with some difficulty, as it was a queer-shaped little creature and held out its arms and legs in all directions. "If I don't take this child away with me," thought Alice, "they're sure to kill it in a day or two. Wouldn't it be murder to leave it behind?" She said the last words out loud and the little thing grunted in reply.

"If you're going to turn into a pig, my dear," said Alice, "I'll have nothing more to do with you. Mind now!"

Alice was just beginning to think to herself, "Now, what am I to do with this creature, when I get it home?" when it grunted again so violently that Alice looked down into its face in some alarm. This time there could be *no* mistake about it—it was neither more nor less than a pig; so she set the little creature down and felt quite relieved to see it trot away quietly into the wood.

Alice was a little startled by seeing the Cheshire-Cat sitting on a bough of a tree a few yards off. The Cat only grinned when it saw her. "Cheshire-Puss," began Alice, rather timidly, "would you please tell me which way I ought to go from here?"

"In *that* direction," the Cat said, waving the right paw round, "lives a Hatter; and in *that* direction," waving the other paw, "lives a March Hare. Visit either you like; they're both mad."

"But I don't want to go among mad people," Alice remarked.

"Oh, you can't help that," said the Cat; "we're all mad here. Do you play croquet with the Queen to-day?"

"I should like it very much," said Alice, "but I haven't been invited yet."

"You'll see me there," said the Cat, and vanished.

Alice had not gone much farther before she came in sight of the house of the March Hare; it was so large a house that she did not like to go near till she had nibbled some more of the left-hand bit of mushroom.

# CHAPTER VII
## A Mad Tea-Party

There was a table set out under a tree in front of the house, and the March Hare and the Hatter were having tea at it; a Dormouse was sitting between them, fast asleep.

The table was a large one, but the three were all crowded together at one corner of it. "No room! No room!" they cried out when they saw Alice coming. "There's *plenty* of room!" said Alice indignantly, and she sat down in a large arm-chair at one end of the table.

The Hatter opened his eyes very wide on hearing this, but all he said was "Why is a raven like a writing-desk?"

"I'm glad they've begun asking riddles—I believe I can guess that," she added aloud.

"Do you mean that you think you can find out the answer to it?" said the March Hare.

"Exactly so," said Alice.

"Then you should say what you mean," the

March Hare went on.

"I do," Alice hastily replied; "at least—at least I mean what I say—that's the same thing, you know."

"You might just as well say," added the Dormouse, which seemed to be talking in its sleep, "that 'I breathe when I sleep' is the same thing as 'I sleep when I breathe!'"

"It *is* the same thing with you," said the Hatter, and he poured a little hot tea upon its nose. The Dormouse shook its head impatiently and said, without opening its eyes, "Of course, of course; just what I was going to remark myself."

"Have you guessed the riddle yet?" the Hatter said, turning to Alice again.

"No, I give it up," Alice replied. "What's the answer?"

"I haven't the slightest idea," said the Hatter.
"Nor I," said the March Hare.

Alice gave a weary sigh. "I think you might do something better with the time," she said, "than wasting it in asking riddles that have no answers."

"Take some more tea," the March Hare said to

Alice, very earnestly.

"I've had nothing yet," Alice replied in an offended tone, "so I can't take more."

"You mean you can't take *less*," said the Hatter; "it's very easy to take *more* than nothing."

At this, Alice got up and walked off. The Dormouse fell asleep instantly and neither of the others took the least notice of her going, though she looked back once or twice; the last time she saw them, they were trying to put the Dormouse into the tea-pot.

"At any rate, I'll never go *there* again!" said Alice, as she picked her way through the wood. "It's the stupidest tea-party I ever was at in all my life!" Just as she said this, she noticed that one of the trees had a door leading right into it. "That's very curious!" she thought. "I think I may as well go in at once." And in she went.

Once more she found herself in the long hall and close to the little glass table. Taking the little golden key, she unlocked the door that led into the garden. Then she set to work nibbling at the mushroom (she had kept a piece of it in her pocket) till she was about a foot high; then she walked down the little passage; and *then* — she found herself at last in the beautiful garden, among the bright flower-beds and the cool fountains.

# CHAPTER VIII
## The Queen's Croquet-Ground

A large rose-tree stood near the entrance of the garden; the roses growing on it were white, but there were three gardeners at it, busily painting them red. Suddenly their eyes chanced to fall upon Alice, as she stood watching them. "Would you tell me, please," said Alice, a little timidly, "why you are painting those roses?"

Five and Seven said nothing, but looked at Two. Two began, in a low voice, "Why, the fact is, you see, Miss, this here ought to have been a *red* rose-tree, and we put a white one in by mistake; and, if the Queen was to find it out, we should all have our heads cut off, you know. So you see, Miss, we're doing our best, afore she comes, to—" At this moment, Five, who had been anxiously looking across the garden, called out, "The Queen! The Queen!" and the three gardeners instantly threw themselves flat upon their faces. There was a sound of many footsteps and Alice looked round, eager to see the Queen.

First came ten soldiers carrying clubs, with their hands and feet at the corners: next the ten courtiers; these were ornamented all over with diamonds. After these came the royal children; there were ten of them, all ornamented with hearts. Next came the guests, mostly Kings and Queens, and among them Alice recognized the White Rabbit. Then followed the Knave of Hearts, carrying the King's crown on a crimson velvet cushion; and last of all this grand procession came THE KING AND THE QUEEN OF HEARTS.

When the procession came opposite to Alice, they all stopped and looked at her, and the Queen said severely, "Who is this?" She said it to the Knave of Hearts, who only bowed and smiled in reply.

"My name is Alice, so please Your Majesty," said Alice very politely; but she added to herself, "Why, they're only a pack of cards, after all!"

"Can you play croquet?" shouted the Queen. The question was evidently meant for Alice.

"Yes!" said Alice loudly.

"Come on, then!" roared the Queen.

"It's—it's a very fine day!" said a timid voice to Alice. She was walking by the White Rabbit, who was peeping anxiously into her face.

"Very," said Alice. "Where's the Duchess?"

"Hush! Hush!" said the Rabbit. "She's under sentence of execution."

"What for?" said Alice.

"She boxed the Queen's ears—" the Rabbit began.

"Get to your places!" shouted the Queen in a voice of thunder, and people began running about in all directions, tumbling up against each other. However, they got settled down in a minute or two, and the game began.

Alice thought she had never seen such a curious croquet-ground in her life; it was all ridges and furrows. The croquet balls were live hedgehogs, and the mallets live flamingos and the soldiers had to double themselves up and stand on their hands and feet, to make the arches.

The players all played at once, without waiting for turns, quarrelling all the while and fighting for the hedgehogs; and in a very short time, the Queen was in a furious passion and went stamping about and shouting, "Off with his head!" or "Off with her head!" about once in a minute.

"They're dreadfully fond of beheading people here," thought Alice; "the great wonder is that there's anyone left alive!"

She was looking about for some way of escape, when she noticed a curious appearance in the air. "It's the Cheshire-Cat," she said to herself; "now I shall have somebody to talk to."

"How are you getting on?" said the Cat.

"I don't think they play at all fairly," Alice said, in a rather complaining tone; "and they all quarrel so dreadfully one can't hear oneself speak—and they don't seem to have any rules in particular."

"How do you like the Queen?" said the Cat in a low voice.

"Not at all," said Alice.

Alice thought she might as well go back and see how the game was going on. So she went off in search of her hedgehog. The hedgehog was engaged in a fight with another hedgehog, which seemed to Alice an excellent opportunity for croqueting one of them with the other; the only difficulty was that her flamingo was gone across to the other side of the garden, where Alice could see it trying, in a helpless sort of way, to fly up into a tree. She caught the flamingo and tucked it away under her arm, that it might not escape again.

Just then Alice ran across the Duchess (who was now out of prison). She tucked her arm affectionately into Alice's and they walked off together. Alice was very glad to find her in such a pleasant temper. She was a little startled, however, when she heard the voice of the Duchess close to her ear. "You're thinking about something, my dear, and that makes you forget to talk."

"The game's going on rather better now," Alice said, by way of keeping up the conversation a little.

"'Tis so," said the Duchess; "and the moral of that is—'Oh, 'tis love, 'tis love that makes the world go round!'"

"Somebody said," Alice whispered, "that it's done by everybody minding his own business!"

"Ah, well! It means much the same thing," said the Duchess, digging her sharp little chin into Alice's shoulder, as she added "and the moral of *that* is—'Take care of the sense and the sounds will take care of themselves.'"

To Alice's great surprise, the Duchess's arm that was linked into hers began to tremble. Alice looked up and there stood the Queen in front of them, with her arms folded, frowning like a thunderstorm!

"Now, I give you fair warning," shouted the Queen, stamping on the ground as she spoke, "either you or your head must be off, and that in about half no time. Take your choice!" The Duchess took her choice, and was gone in a moment.

"Let's go on with the game," the Queen said to Alice; and Alice was too much frightened to say a word, but slowly followed her back to the croquet-ground.

All the time they were playing, the Queen never left off quarreling with the other players and shouting, "Off with his head!" or "Off with her head!" By the end of half an hour or so, all the players, except the King, the Queen and Alice, were in custody of the soldiers and under sentence of execution.

Then the Queen left off, quite out of breath, and walked away with Alice.

Alice heard the King say in a low voice to the company generally, "You are all pardoned."

Suddenly the cry "The Trial's beginning!" was heard in the distance, and Alice ran along with the others.

# CHAPTER IX
## The Mock Turtle's Story

You can't think how glad I am to see you again, you dear old thing!" said the Duchess, as she tucked her arm affectionately into Alice's, and they walked off together.

Alice was very glad to find her in such a pleasant temper, and thought to herself that perhaps it was only the pepper that had made her so savage when they met in the kitchen.

"When I'm a Duchess," she said to herself (not in a very hopeful tone though), "I won't have any pepper in my kitchen at all. Soup does very well without—Maybe it's always pepper that makes people hot-tempered," she went on, very much pleased at having found out a new kind of rule, "and vinegar that makes them sour—and camomile that makes them bitter—and—barley-sugar and such things that make children sweet-tempered. I only wish people knew that: then they wouldn't be so stingy about it, you know——"

She had quite forgotten the Duchess by this time, and was a little startled when she heard her voice close to her ear. "You're thinking about something, my dear, and that makes you forget to talk. I can't tell you just now what the moral of that is, but I shall remember it in a bit."

"Perhaps it hasn't one," Alice ventured to remark.

"Tut, tut, child!" said the Duchess. "Every thing's got a moral, if only you can find it." And she squeezed herself up closer to Alice's side as she spoke.

Alice did not much like her keeping so close to her: first, because the Duchess was very ugly; and secondly, because she was exactly the right height to rest her chin on Alice's shoulder, and it was an uncomfortably sharp chin. However, she did not like to be rude, so she bore it as well as she could. "The game's going on rather better now," she said, by way of keeping up the conversation a little.

"'Tis so," said the Duchess: "and the moral of that is—'Oh, 'tis love, 'tis love, that makes the world go round!'"

"Somebody said," Alice whispered, "that it's done by everybody minding their own business!"

"Ah, well! It means much the same thing," said the Duchess, digging her sharp little chin into Alice's shoulder as she added, "and the moral of that is—'Take care of the sense, and the sounds will take care of themselves.'"

"How fond she is of finding morals in things!" Alice thought to herself.

"I dare say you're wondering why I don't put my arm round your waist," the Duchess said after a pause: "the reason is, that I'm doubtful about the temper of your flamingo. Shall I try the experiment?"

"He might bite," Alice cautiously replied, not feeling at all anxious to have the experiment tried.

"Very true," said the Duchess: "flamingoes and mustard both bite. And the moral of that is—'Birds of a feather flock together.'"

"Only mustard isn't a bird," Alice remarked.

"Right, as usual," said the Duchess: "what a clear way you have of putting things!"

"It's a mineral, I think," said Alice.

"Of course it is," said the Duchess, who seemed ready to agree to everything that Alice said: "there's a large mustard-mine near here. And the moral of that is—'The more there is of mine, the less there is of yours.'"

"Oh, I know!" exclaimed Alice, who had not attended to this last remark. "It's a vegetable. It doesn't look like one, but it is."

"I quite agree with you," said the Duchess; "and the moral of that is—'Be what you would seem to be'—or if you'd like it put more simply—'Never imagine yourself not to be otherwise than what it might appear to others that what you were or might have been was not otherwise than what you had been would have appeared to them to be otherwise.'"

"I think I should understand that better," Alice said very politely, "if I had it written down: but I can't quite follow it as you say it."

"That's nothing to what I could say if I chose," the Duchess replied, in a pleased tone.

"Pray don't trouble yourself to say it any longer than that," said Alice.

"Oh, don't talk about trouble!" said the Duchess. "I make you a present of everything I've said as yet."

"A cheap sort of present!" thought Alice. "I'm glad they don't give birthday presents like that!" But she did not venture to say it out loud.

"Thinking again?" the Duchess asked with another dig of her sharp little chin.

"I've a right to think," said Alice sharply, for she was beginning to feel a little worried.

"Just about as much right," said the Duchess, "as pigs have to fly; and the m——"

But here, to Alice's great surprise, the Duchess's voice died away, even in the middle of her favourite word "moral," and the arm that was linked into hers began to tremble. Alice looked up, and there stood the Queen in front of them, with her arms folded, frowning like a thunderstorm.

"A fine day, your Majesty!" the Duchess began in a low, weak voice.

"Now, I give you fair warning," shouted the Queen, stamping on the ground as she spoke; "either you or your head must be off, and that in about half no time! Take your choice!"

The Duchess took her choice, and was gone in a moment.

"Let's go on with the game," the Queen said to Alice; and Alice was too much frightened to say a word, but slowly followed her back to the croquet-ground.

The other guests had taken advantage of the Queen's absence, and were resting in the shade: however, the moment they saw her, they hurried back to the game, the Queen merely remarking that a moment's delay would cost them their lives.

All the time they were playing the Queen never left off quarrelling with the other players, and shouting "Off with his head!" or, "Off with her head!"

Those whom she sentenced were taken into custody by the soldiers, who of course had to leave off being arches to do this, so that by the end of half an hour or so there were no arches left, and all the players, except the King, the Queen, and Alice, were in custody and under sentence of execution.

Then the Queen left off, quite out of breath, and said to Alice, "Have you seen the Mock Turtle yet?"

"No," said Alice. "I don't even know what a Mock Turtle is."

"It's the thing Mock Turtle Soup is made from," said the Queen.

"I never saw one, or heard of one," said Alice.

"Come on then," said the Queen, "and he shall tell you his history."

As they walked off together, Alice heard the King say in a low voice, to the company generally, "You are all pardoned." "Come, that's a good thing!" she said to herself, for she had felt quite unhappy at the number of executions the Queen had ordered.

They very soon came upon a Gryphon, lying fast asleep in the sun. (If you don't know what a Gryphon is, look at the picture.) "Up, lazy thing!" said the Queen, "and take this young lady to see the Mock Turtle, and to hear his history. I must go back and see after some executions I have ordered," and she walked off, leaving Alice alone with the Gryphon. Alice did not quite like the look of the creature, but on the whole she thought it would be quite as safe to stay with it as to go after that savage Queen: so she waited.

The Gryphon sat up and rubbed its eyes: then it watched the Queen till she was out of sight: then it chuckled. "What fun!" said the Gryphon, half to itself, half to Alice.

"What is the fun?" said Alice.

"Why, she," said the Gryphon. "It's all her fancy, that: they never executes nobody, you know. Come on!"

"Everybody says 'come on!' here," thought Alice, as she went slowly after it: "I never was so ordered about in my life, never!"

They had not gone far before they saw the Mock Turtle in the distance, sitting sad and lonely on a little ledge of rock, and, as they came nearer, Alice could hear him sighing as if his heart would break. She pitied him deeply. "What is his sorrow?" she asked the Gryphon, and the Gryphon answered, very nearly in the same words as before, "It's all his fancy, that: he hasn't got no sorrow, you know. Come on!"

So they went up to the Mock Turtle, who looked at them with large eyes full of tears, but said nothing.

"This here young lady," said the Gryphon, "she wants to know your history, she do."

"I'll tell it her," said the Mock Turtle in a deep, hollow tone; "sit down, both of you, and don't speak a word till I've finished."

So they sat down, and nobody spoke for some minutes. Alice thought to herself, "I don't see how he can ever finish, if he doesn't begin." But she waited patiently.

"Once," said the Mock Turtle at last, with a deep sigh, "I was a real Turtle."

These words were followed by a very long silence, broken only by an occasional exclamation of "Hjckrrh!" from the Gryphon, and the constant heavy sobbing of the Mock Turtle. Alice was very nearly getting up and saying "Thank you, sir, for your interesting story," but she could not help thinking there must be more to come, so she sat still and said nothing.

"When we were little," the Mock Turtle went on at last, more calmly, though still sobbing a little now and then, "we went to school in the sea. The master was an old Turtle—we used to call him Tortoise——"

"Why did you call him Tortoise, if he wasn't one?" Alice asked.

"We called him Tortoise because he taught us," said the Mock Turtle angrily: "really you are very dull!"

"You ought to be ashamed of yourself for asking such a simple question," added the Gryphon; and then they both sat silent and looked at poor Alice, who felt ready to sink into the earth. At last the Gryphon said to the Mock Turtle, "Drive on, old fellow. Don't be all day about it!" and he went on in these words:

"Yes, we went to school in the sea, though you mayn't believe it——"

"I never said I didn't!" interrupted Alice.

"You did," said the Mock Turtle.

"Hold your tongue!" added the Gryphon, before Alice could speak again. The Mock Turtle went on:—

"We had the best of educations—in fact, we went to school every day——"

"I've been to a day-school, too," said Alice; "you needn't be so proud as all that."

"With extras?" asked the Mock Turtle a little anxiously.

"Yes," said Alice, "we learned French and music."

"And washing?" said the Mock Turtle.

"Certainly not!" said Alice indignantly.

"Ah! then yours wasn't a really good school," said the Mock Turtle in a tone of relief. "Now at ours they had at the end of the bill, 'French, music, and washing—extra.'"

"You couldn't have wanted it much," said Alice; "living at the bottom of the sea."

"I couldn't afford to learn it," said the Mock Turtle with a sigh. "I only took the regular course."

"What was that?" inquired Alice.

"Reeling and Writhing, of course, to begin with," the Mock Turtle replied; "and then the different branches of Arithmetic—Ambition, Dist raction, Uglification, and Derision."

"I never heard of 'Uglification,'" Alice ventured to say. "What is it?"

The Gryphon lifted up both its paws in surprise. "Never heard of uglifying!" it exclaimed. "You know what to beautify is, I suppose?"

"Yes," said Alice doubtfully: "it means—to—make—anything—prettier."

"Well, then," the Gryphon went on, "if you don't know what to uglify is, you are a simpleton."

Alice did not feel encouraged to ask any more questions about it, so she turned to the Mock Turtle and said, "What else had you to learn?"

"Well, there was Mystery," the Mock Turtle replied, counting off the subjects on his flappers, "—Mystery, ancient and modern, with Seaography: then Drawling—the Drawling-master was an old conger-eel, that used to come once a week: he taught us Drawling, Stretching, and Fainting in Coils."

"What was that like?" said Alice.

"Well, I can't show it you myself," the Mock Turtle said: "I'm too stiff. And the Gryphon never learnt it."

"Hadn't time," said the Gryphon: "I went to the Classical master, though. He was an old crab, he was."

"I never went to him," the Mock Turtle said with a sigh: "he taught Laughing and Grief, they used to say."

"So he did, so he did," said the Gryphon, sighing in his turn; and both creatures hid their faces in their paws.

"And how many hours a day did you do lessons?" said Alice, in a hurry to change the subject.

"Ten hours the first day," said the Mock Turtle: "nine the next, and so on."

"What a curious plan!" exclaimed Alice.

"That's the reason they're called lessons," the Gryphon remarked: "because they lessen from day to day."

This was quite a new idea to Alice, and she thought over it a little before she made her next remark. "Then the eleventh day must have been a holiday."

"Of course it was," said the Mock Turtle.

"And how did you manage on the twelfth?" Alice went on eagerly.

"That's enough about lessons," the Gryphon interrupted in a very decided tone: "tell her something about the games now."

# CHAPTER X
## The Lobster Quadrille

The Mock Turtle sighed deeply, and drew the back of one flapper across his eyes. He looked at Alice, and tried to speak, but, for a minute or two, sobs choked his voice. "Same as if he had a bone in his throat," said the Gryphon: and it set to work shaking him and punching him in the back. At last the Mock Turtle recovered his voice, and, with tears running down his cheeks, went on again:

"You may not have lived much under the sea—" ("I haven't," said Alice) "and perhaps you were never even introduced to a lobster—" (Alice began to say "I once tasted——" but checked herself hastily, and said "No, never,) "—so you can have no idea what a delightful thing a Lobster Quadrille is!"

"No, indeed," said Alice. "What sort of a dance is it?"

"Why," said the Gryphon, "you first form into a

line along the sea-shore——"

"Two lines!" cried the Mock Turtle. "Seals, turtles, and so on; then, when you've cleared the jelly-fish out of the way——"

"That generally takes some time," interrupted the Gryphon.

"—you advance twice——"

"Each with a lobster as a partner!" cried the Gryphon.

"Of course," the Mock Turtle said: "advance twice, set to partners——"

"—change lobsters, and retire in same order," continued the Gryphon.

"Then, you know," the Mock Turtle went on, "you throw the——"

"The lobsters!" shouted the Gryphon, with a bound into the air.

"—as far out to sea as you can——"

"Swim, after them!" screamed the Gryphon.

"Turn a somersault in the sea!" cried the Mock Turtle, capering wildly about.

"Change lobsters again!" yelled the Gryphon.

"Back to land again, and—that's all the first figure," said the Mock Turtle, suddenly dropping his voice; and the two creatures, who had been jumping about like mad things all this time, sat down again very sadly and quietly, and looked at Alice.

"It must be a very pretty dance," said Alice, timidly.

"Would you like to see a little of it?" said the Mock Turtle.

"Very much indeed," said Alice.

"Come, let's try the first figure!" said the Mock Turtle to the Gryphon. "We can do it without lobsters, you know. Which shall sing?"

"Oh, you sing," said the Gryphon. "I've forgotten the words."

So they began solemnly dancing round and round Alice, every now and then treading on her toes when they passed too close, and waving their forepaws to mark the time, while the Mock Turtle sang this, very slowly and sadly:—

"Will you walk a little faster?" said a whiting to a snail,

"There's a porpoise close behind us, and he's

treading on my tail.

See how eagerly the lobsters and the turtles all advance!

They are waiting on the shingle—will you come and join the dance?

Will you, won't you, will you, won't you, will you join the dance?

Will you, won't you, will you, won't you, won't you join the dance?


"You can really have no notion how delightful it will be,

When they take us up and throw us, with the lobsters, out to sea!"

But the snail replied: "Too far, too far!" and gave a look askance—

Said he thanked the whiting kindly, but he would not join the dance.

Would not, could not, would not, could not, would not join the dance.

Would not, could not, would not, could not, could not join the dance.

"What matters it how far we go?" his scary friend replied;

"There is another shore, you know, upon the other side.

The further off from England the nearer is to France—

Then turn not pale, beloved snail, but come and join the dance.

Will you, won't you, will you, won't you, will you join the dance?

Will you, won't you, will you, won't you, won't you join the dance?"


"Thank you, it's a very interesting dance to watch," said Alice, feeling very glad that it was over at last: "and I do so like that curious song about the whiting!"

"Oh, as to the whiting," said the Mock Turtle, "they—you've seen them, of course?"

"Yes," said Alice, "I've often seen them at dinn——" she checked herself hastily.

"I don't know where Dinn may be," said the Mock Turtle, "but if you've seen them so often, of course you know what they're like."

"I believe so," Alice replied thoughtfully. "They have their tails in their mouths—and they're all over crumbs."

"You're wrong about the crumbs," said the Mock Turtle: "crumbs would all wash off in the sea. But they have their tails in their mouths; and the reason is—" here the Mock Turtle yawned and shut his eyes. "Tell her about the reason and all that," he said to the Gryphon.

"The reason is," said the Gryphon, "that they would go with the lobsters to the dance. So they got thrown out to sea. So they had to fall a long way. So they got their tails fast in their mouths. So they couldn't get them out again. That's all."

"Thank you," said Alice. "It's very interesting. I never knew so much about a whiting before."

"I can tell you more than that, if you like," said the Gryphon. "Do you know why it's called a whiting?"

"I never thought about it," said Alice. "Why?"

"It does the boots and shoes," the Gryphon replied very solemnly.

Alice was thoroughly puzzled. "Does the boots and shoes!" she repeated in a wondering tone.

"Why, what are your shoes done with?" said the Gryphon. "I mean, what makes them so shiny?"

Alice looked down at them, and considered a little before she gave her answer. "They're done with blacking, I believe."

"Boots and shoes under the sea," the Gryphon went on in a deep voice, "are done with whiting. Now you know."

"And what are they made of?" Alice asked in a tone of great curiosity.

"Soles and eels, of course," the Gryphon replied rather impatiently: "any shrimp could have told you that."

"If I'd been the whiting," said Alice, whose thoughts were still running on the song, "I'd have said to the porpoise, 'Keep back, please: we don't want you with us!'"

"They were obliged to have him with them," the Mock Turtle said: "no wise fish would go anywhere without a porpoise."

"Wouldn't it really?" said Alice in a tone of great surprise.

"Of course not," said the Mock Turtle: "why, if a fish came to me, and told me he was going a journey, I should say, 'With what porpoise?'"

"Don't you mean 'purpose'?" said Alice.

"I mean what I say," the Mock Turtle replied in an offended tone. And the Gryphon added, "Come, let's hear some of your adventures."

"I could tell you my adventures—beginning from this morning," said Alice a little timidly: "but it's no use going back to yesterday, because I was a different person then."

"Explain all that," said the Mock Turtle.

"No, no! The adventures first," said the Gryphon in an impatient tone: "explanations take such a dreadful time."

So Alice began telling them her adventures from the time when she first saw the White Rabbit. She was a little nervous about it just at first, the two creatures got so close to her, one on each side, and opened their eyes and mouths so very wide, but she gained courage as she went on. Her listeners were perfectly quiet till she got to the part about her repeating "You are old, Father William," to the Caterpillar, and the words all coming different, and then the Mock Turtle drew a long breath, and said, "That's very curious."

"It's all about as curious as it can be," said the Gryphon.

"It all came different!" the Mock Turtle repeated thoughtfully. "I should like to hear her repeat something now. Tell her to begin." He looked at the Gryphon as if he thought it had some kind of authority over Alice.

"Stand up and repeat ''Tis the voice of the sluggard,'" said the Gryphon.

"How the creatures order one about, and make one repeat lessons!" thought Alice. "I might as well be at school at once." However, she got up, and began to repeat it, but her head was so full of the Lobster Quadrille, that she hardly knew what she was saying, and the words came very queer indeed:—

"'Tis the voice of the Lobster; I heard him

declare,

'You have baked me too brown, I must sugar my hair.'

As a duck with its eyelids, so he with his nose Trims his belt and his buttons, and turns out his toes.

When the sands are all dry, he is gay as a lark, And will talk in contemptuous tones of the Shark:

But, when the tide rises and sharks are around, His voice has a timid and tremulous sound."

"That's different from what I used to say when I was a child," said the Gryphon.

"Well, I never heard it before," said the Mock Turtle: "but it sounds uncommon nonsense."

Alice said nothing; she had sat down with her face in her hands, wondering if anything would ever happen in a natural way again.

"I should like to have it explained," said the Mock Turtle.

"She ca'n't explain it," hastily said the Gryphon. "Go on with the next verse."

"But about his toes?" the Mock Turtle persisted. "How could he turn them out with his nose, you know?"

"It's the first position in dancing," Alice said; but was dreadfully puzzled by the whole thing, and longed to change the subject.

"Go on with the next verse," the Gryphon repeated: "it begins 'I passed by his garden.'"

Alice did not dare to disobey, though she felt sure it would all come wrong, and she went on in a trembling voice:

"I passed by his garden, and marked, with one eye,
How the Owl and the Panther were sharing a pie:
The Panther took pie-crust, and gravy, and meat,
While the Owl had the dish as its share of the treat.
When the pie was all finished, the Owl, as a boon,
Was kindly permitted to pocket the spoon:

While the Panther received knife and fork with a growl,
And concluded the banquet by——"

"What is the use of repeating all that stuff," the Mock Turtle interrupted, "if you don't explain it as you go on? It's by far the most confusing thing I ever heard!"

"Yes, I think you'd better leave off," said the Gryphon: and Alice was only too glad to do so.

"Shall we try another figure of the Lobster Quadrille?" the Gryphon went on. "Or would you like the Mock Turtle to sing you another song?"

"Oh, a song, please, if the Mock Turtle would be so kind," Alice replied, so eagerly that the Gryphon said, in a rather offended tone, "H'm! No accounting for tastes! Sing her 'Turtle Soup,' will you, old fellow?"

The Mock Turtle sighed deeply, and began, in a voice choked with sobs, to sing this:—

"Beautiful Soup, so rich and green,
Waiting in a hot tureen!

Who for such dainties would not stoop?
Soup of the evening, beautiful Soup!
Soup of the evening, beautiful Soup!

Soo—oop of the e—e—evening,
"Beautiful Soup! Who cares for fish,
Game, or any other dish?
Who would not give all else for two
Pennyworth only of beautiful Soup?
Pennyworth only of beautiful Soup?

Beau—ootiful Soo—oop!

Soo—oop of the e—e—evening,

Beautiful, beauti—FUL SOUP!"

"Chorus again!" cried the Gryphon, and the Mock Turtle had just begun to repeat it, when a cry of "The trial's beginning!" was heard in the distance.

"Come on!" cried the Gryphon, and, taking Alice by the hand, it hurried off, without waiting for the end of the song.

"What trial is it?" Alice panted as she ran; but the Gryphon only answered "Come on!" and ran

the faster, while more and more faintly came,
carried on the breeze that followed them, the
melancholy words:—

"Soo—oop of the e—e—evening,

Beautiful, beautiful Soup!"

# CHAPTER XI
# Who Stole the Tarts?

The King and Queen of Hearts were seated on their throne when they arrived, with a great crowd assembled about them—all sorts of little birds and beasts, as well as the whole pack of cards: the Knave was standing before them, in chains, with a soldier on each side to guard him; and near the King was the White Rabbit, with a trumpet in one hand and a scroll of parchment in the other. In the very middle of the court was a table, with a large dish of tarts upon it. "I wish they'd get the trial done," Alice thought, "and hand round the refreshments!"

The judge, by the way, was the King and he wore his crown over his great wig. "That's the jury-box," thought Alice; "and those twelve creatures (some were animals and some were birds) I suppose they are the jurors."

Just then the White Rabbit cried out "Silence in the court!"

"Herald, read the accusation!" said the King.

On this, the White Rabbit blew three blasts on the trumpet, then unrolled the parchment-scroll and read as follows:

"The Queen of Hearts, she made some tarts,

All on a summer day;

The Knave of Hearts, he stole those tarts And

took them quite away!"

"Call the first witness," said the King; and the White Rabbit blew three blasts on the trumpet and called out, "First witness!"

The first witness was the Hatter. He came in with a teacup in one hand and a piece of bread and butter in the other.

"You ought to have finished," said the King. "When did you begin?"

The Hatter looked at the March Hare, who had followed him into the court, arm in arm with the Dormouse. "Fourteenth of March, I *think* it was," he said.

"Give your evidence," said the King, "and don't

be nervous, or I'll have you executed on the spot."

This did not seem to encourage the witness at all; he kept shifting from one foot to the other, looking uneasily at the Queen, and, in his confusion, he bit a large piece out of his teacup instead of the bread and butter.

Just at this moment Alice felt a very curious sensation—she was beginning to grow larger again.

The miserable Hatter dropped his teacup and bread and butter and went down on one knee. "I'm a poor man, Your Majesty," he began.

"You're a *very* poor *speaker*," said the King.

"You may go," said the King, and the Hatter hurriedly left the court.

"Call the next witness!" said the King.

The next witness was the Duchess's cook. She carried the pepper-box in her hand and the people near the door began sneezing all at once.

"Give your evidence," said the King.

"Sha'n't," said the cook.

The King looked anxiously at the White Rabbit, who said, in a low voice, "Your Majesty must cross-examine *this* witness."

"Well, if I must, I must," the King said. "What are tarts made of?"

"Pepper, mostly," said the cook.

For some minutes the whole court was in confusion and by the time they had settled down again, the cook had disappeared.

"Never mind!" said the King, "call the next witness."

Alice watched the White Rabbit as he fumbled over the list. Imagine her surprise when he read out, at the top of his shrill little voice, the name "Alice!"

# CHAPTER XII
## Alice's Evidence

"Here!" cried Alice. She jumped up in such a hurry that she tipped over the jury-box, upsetting all the jurymen on to the heads of the crowd below.

"Oh, I *beg* your pardon!" she exclaimed in a tone of great dismay.

"The trial cannot proceed," said the King, "until all the jurymen are back in their proper places- *all*," he repeated with great emphasis, looking hard at Alice.

"What do you know about this business?" the King said to Alice.

"Nothing whatever," said Alice.

The King then read from his book: "Rule forty-two. *All persons more than a mile high to leave the court.*"

"*I'm* not a mile high," said Alice.

"Nearly two miles high," said the Queen.

"Well, I sha'n't go, at any rate," said Alice.

The King turned pale and shut his note-book hastily. "Consider your verdict," he said to the jury, in a low, trembling voice.

"There's more evidence to come yet, please Your Majesty," said the White Rabbit, jumping up in a great hurry. "This paper has just been picked up. It seems to be a letter written by the prisoner to—to somebody." He unfolded the paper as he spoke and added, "It isn't a letter, after all; it's a set of verses."

"Please, Your Majesty," said the Knave, "I didn't write it and they can't prove that I did; there's no name signed at the end."

"You *must* have meant some mischief, or else you'd have signed your name like an honest man," said the King. There was a general clapping of hands at this.

"Read them," he added, turning to the White Rabbit.

There was dead silence in the court whilst the White Rabbit read out the verses.

"That's the most important piece of evidence we've heard yet," said the King.

"*I* don't believe there's an atom of meaning in it," ventured Alice.

"If there's no meaning in it," said the King, "that saves a world of trouble, you know, as we needn't try to find any. Let the jury consider their verdict."

"No, no!" said the Queen. "Sentence first—verdict afterwards."

"Stuff and nonsense!" said Alice loudly. "The idea of having the sentence first!"

"Hold your tongue!" said the Queen, turning purple.

"I won't!" said Alice.

"Off with her head!" the Queen shouted at the top of her voice. Nobody moved.

"Who cares for *you*?" said Alice (she had grown to her full size by this time). "You're nothing but a pack of cards!"

At this, the whole pack rose up in the air and came flying down upon her; she gave a little scream, half of fright and half of anger, and tried to beat them off, and found herself lying on the bank, with her head in the lap of her sister, who was gently brushing away some dead leaves that had fluttered down from the trees upon her face.

"Wake up, Alice dear!" said her sister. "Why, what a long sleep you've had!"

"Oh, I've had such a curious dream!" said Alice. And she told her sister, as well as she could remember them, all these strange adventures of hers that you have just been reading about. Alice got up and ran off, thinking while she ran, as well she might, what a wonderful dream it had been.

THE END

# 📚 나만의 리뷰 *and* 명문장

# 거울 나라의 앨리스

## Through The Looking-Rrass

루이스 캐럴 지음

## ❖ 『거울 나라의 앨리스』 줄거리

**1장:** 어느 날, 거실에서 거울을 보던 앨리스는 문득 거울 속의 집은 어떨지 궁금해진다. 앨리스가 거울에 발을 집어넣자 몸이 거울 속으로 쑥 들어가게 된다.

**2장:** 거울 나라로 들어온 앨리스는 살아 있는 꽃들이 있는 정원으로 간다. 꽃들과 대화를 나누던 앨리스는 붉은 여왕을 만나게 되고 진짜 여왕이 되는 법을 배운다. 졸(pawn)에서 여왕(queen)이 되기 위해 체스판처럼 구획이 나눠진 곳을 거쳐야 한다.

**3장:** 기차를 탄 앨리스는 말하는 곤충들을 만나 이야기를 나누고, 들어가면 그 속에서는 모든 것들이 이름을 잃게 되는 숲으로 들어간다.

**4장:** 숲 속에서 앨리스는 쌍둥이 형제 트위들덤과 트위들디를 만난다. 이들은 앨리스가 붉은 왕의 꿈속에서만 존재하는 환상일 거라고 주장하고, 앨리스는 자신이 진짜 살아있는 사람이라고 주장한다.

**5장:** 앨리스는 날아오는 숄을 잡아 주인인 하얀 여왕에게 건네준다. 하얀 여왕은 거꾸로 살고 있어서, 상처가 나기 전에 소리를 지르고, 벌을 받은 다음에 죄를 짓게 한다. 하얀 여왕과 이야기를 나누던 중, 갑자기 여왕은 사라지고 앨리스는 양의 가게에 와 있다.

**6장:** 양에게 달걀을 산 앨리스는 거대한 달걀처럼 생긴 험프티 덤프티를 만난다. 높은 담장에 앉아 잘난 척을 하던 험프티 덤프티는 앨리스가 떠난 뒤 떨어져 깨져 버리고 만다.

**7장:** 앨리스는 숲 속에서 걸핏하면 넘어지는 하얀 왕과 병사들을 만난다. 앨리스는 사자와 유니콘이 왕관을 놓고 싸운다는 소식을 듣고, 그들을 만나러 간다.

**8장:** 갑자기 모든 것이 사라지고 붉은 기사와 하얀 기사가 등장해 전투를 벌인다. 전투를 마친 하얀 기사는 앨리스에게 자신의 발명품들을 자랑하며, 앨리스를 숲의 끝까지 데려다 준다.

**9장:** 마지막 실개천을 건너간 앨리스는 여왕이 된다. 그러나 붉은 여왕은 앨리스가 시험에 통과해야 진짜 여왕이 된다고 말하며, 앨리스를 만찬에 초대한다. 앨리스는 붉은 여왕과 하얀 여왕 사이에 앉아서 온갖 이상한 소동에 휘말린다.

**10장:** 붉은 여왕의 장난에 화가 난 앨리스는 그녀를 잡고 마구 흔든다. 붉은 여왕의 얼굴은 점점 작아지고 눈은 점점 초록빛이 되어 간다.

**11장:** 그리고 앨리스의 눈 앞에는 새끼 고양이가 있었다.

**12장:** 잠에서 깬 앨리스는 모든 것이 꿈이었음을 깨닫는다. 앨리스는 고양이들에게 누가 꿈을 꾼 건지 생각해보자고 말한다.

# CONTENTS

### CHAPTER I
Looking-Glass house
*108*

### CHAPTER II
The Garden of Live Flowers
*126*

### CHAPTER III
Looking-Glass Insects
*142*

### CHAPTER IV
Tweedledum And Tweedledee
*158*

### CHAPTER V
Wool and Water
*178*

### CHAPTER VI
Humpty Dumpty
*196*

**CHAPTER VII**

The Lion and the Unicorn

*216*

**CHAPTER VIII**

'It's my own Invention'

*232*

**CHAPTER IX**

Queen Alice

*255*

**CHAPTER X**

Shaking

*280*

**CHAPTER XI**

Waking

*281*

**CHAPTER XII**

Which Dreamed it?

*282*

# CHAPTER I

## Looking-Glass house

One thing was certain, that the WHITE kitten had had nothing to do with it:—it was the black kitten's fault entirely. For the white kitten had been having its face washed by the old cat for the last quarter of an hour (and bearing it pretty well, considering); so you see that it COULDN'T have had any hand in the mischief.

The way Dinah washed her children's faces was this: first she held the poor thing down by its ear with one paw, and then with the other paw she rubbed its face all over, the wrong way, beginning at the nose: and just now, as I said, she was hard at work on the white kitten, which was lying quite still and trying to purr—no doubt feeling that it was all meant for its good.

But the black kitten had been finished with earlier in the afternoon, and so, while Alice was sitting curled up in a corner of the great armchair, half talking to herself and half asleep, the kitten had been having a grand game of romps with the ball of worsted Alice had been trying to wind up, and had been rolling it up and down till it had all come undone again; and there it was, spread over the hearth-rug, all knots and tangles, with the kitten running after its own tail in the middle.

'Oh, you wicked little thing!' cried Alice, catching up the kitten, and giving it a little kiss to make it understand that it was in disgrace. 'Really, Dinah ought to have taught you better manners! You OUGHT, Dinah, you know you ought!' she added, looking reproachfully at the old cat, and speaking in as cross a voice as she could manage—and then she scrambled back into the arm-chair, taking the kitten and the worsted with her, and began winding up the ball again. But she didn't get on very fast, as she was talking all the time, sometimes to the kitten, and sometimes to herself. Kitty sat very demurely on her knee, pretending to watch the progress of the winding, and now and then putting out one paw and gently touching the ball, as if it would be glad to help, if it might.

'Do you know what to-morrow is, Kitty?' Alice began. 'You'd have guessed if you'd been up in the window with me—only Dinah was making you tidy, so you couldn't. I was watching the boys getting in sticks for the bonfire—and it wants plenty of sticks, Kitty! Only it got so cold, and it snowed so, they had to leave off. Never mind, Kitty, we'll go and see the bonfire to-morrow.' Here Alice wound two or three turns of the worsted round the kitten's neck, just to see how it would look: this led to a scramble, in which the ball rolled down upon the floor, and yards and yards of it got unwound again.

'Do you know, I was so angry, Kitty,' Alice went on as soon as they were comfortably settled again, 'when I saw all the mischief you had been doing, I was very nearly opening the window, and putting you out into the snow! And you'd have deserved it, you little mischievous darling! What have you got to say for yourself? Now don't interrupt me!' she went on, holding up one finger. 'I'm going to tell you all your faults. Number one: you squeaked twice while Dinah was washing your face this morning. Now you can't deny it, Kitty: I heard you! What's that you say?' (pretending that the kitten was speaking.) 'Her paw went into your eye? Well, that's YOUR fault, for keeping your eyes open—if you'd shut them tight up, it wouldn't have happened. Now don't make any more excuses, but listen! Number two: you pulled Snowdrop away by the tail just as I had put down the saucer of milk before her! What, you were thirsty, were you? How do you know she wasn't thirsty too? Now for number three: you unwound every bit of the worsted while I wasn't looking!

'That's three faults, Kitty, and you've not been punished for any of them yet. You know I'm saving up all your punishments for Wednesday week—Suppose they had saved up all MY punishments!' she went on, talking more to herself than the kitten. 'What WOULD they do at the end of a year? I should be sent to prison, I suppose, when the day came. Or—let me see—suppose each punishment was to be going without a dinner: then, when the miserable day came, I should have to go without fifty dinners at once! Well, I shouldn't mind THAT much! I'd far rather go without them than eat them!

'do you hear the snow against the window-panes, Kitty? How nice and soft it sounds! Just as if some one was kissing the window all over outside. I wonder if the snow LOVES the trees and fields, that it kisses them so gently? And then it covers them up snug, you know, with a white quilt; and perhaps it says, "Go to sleep, darlings, till the summer comes again." And when they wake up in the summer, Kitty, they dress them-selves all in green, and dance about—whenever the wind blows—oh, that's very pretty!' cried Alice, dropping the ball of worsted to clap her hands. 'And I do so WISH it was true!' I'm sure the woods look sleepy in the autumn, when the leaves are getting brown.

'Kitty, can you play chess? Now, don't smile, my dear, I'm asking it seriously. Because, when we were playing just now, you watched just as if you understood it: and when I said "Check!" you purred! Well, it WAS a nice check, Kitty, and re-ally I might have won, if it hadn't been for that nasty Knight, that came wiggling down among my pieces. Kitty, dear, let's pretend—' And here I wish I could tell you half the things Alice used to say, beginning with her favourite phrase 'Let's pretend.' She had had quite a long argument with her sister only the day before—all because Alice had begun with 'Let's pretend we're kings and queens;' and her sister, who liked being very exact, had argued that they couldn't, because there were only two of them, and Alice had been reduced at last to say, 'Well, YOU can be one of them then, and I'll be all the rest.' And once she had really frightened her old nurse by shouting suddenly in her ear, 'Nurse! Do let's pretend that I'm a hungry hyaena, and you're a bone.'

But this is taking us away from Alice's speech to the kitten. 'Let's pretend that you're the Red Queen, Kitty! Do you know, I think if you sat up and folded your arms, you'd look exactly like her. Now do try, there's a dear!' And Alice got the Red Queen off the table, and set it up before the kitten as a model for it to imitate: however, the thing didn't succeed, principally, Alice said, because the kitten wouldn't fold its arms properly. So, to punish it, she held it up to the Looking-glass, that it might see how sulky it was—'and if you're not good directly,' she added, 'I'll put you through into Looking-glass House. How would you like THAT?'

'Now, if you'll only attend, Kitty, and not talk so much, I'll tell you all my ideas about Looking-glass House. First, there's the room you can see through the glass—that's just the same as our drawing room, only the things go the other way. I can see all of it when I get upon a chair—all but the bit behind the fireplace. Oh! I do so wish I could see THAT bit! I want so much to know whether they've a fire in the winter: you never CAN tell, you know, unless our fire smokes, and then smoke comes up in that room too—but that may be only pretence, just to make it look as if they had a fire. Well then, the books are something like our books, only the words go the wrong way; I know that, because I've held up one of our books to the glass, and then they hold up one in the other room.

'How would you like to live in Looking-glass House, Kitty? I wonder if they'd give you milk in there? Perhaps Looking-glass milk isn't good to drink—But oh, Kitty! now we come to the passage. You can just see a little PEEP of the passage in Looking-glass House, if you leave the door of our drawing-room wide open: and it's very like our passage as far as you can see, only you know it may be quite different on beyond. Oh, Kitty! how nice it would be if we could only get through into Looking-glass House! I'm sure it's got, oh! such beautiful things in it! Let's pretend there's a way of getting through into it, somehow, Kitty. Let's pretend the glass has got all soft like gauze, so that we can get through. Why, it's turning into a sort of mist now, I declare! It'll be easy enough to get through—' She was up on the chimney-piece while she said this, though she hardly knew how she had got there. And certainly the glass WAS beginning to melt away, just like a bright silvery mist.

In another moment Alice was through the glass, and had jumped lightly down into the Looking-glass room. The very first thing she did was to look whether there was a fire in the fireplace, and she was quite pleased to find that there was a real one, blazing away as brightly as the one she had left behind. 'So I shall be as warm here as I was in the old room,' thought Alice: 'warmer, in fact, because there'll be no one here to scold me away from the fire. Oh, what fun it'll be, when they see me through the glass in here, and can't get at me!'

Then she began looking about, and noticed that what could be seen from the old room was quite common and uninteresting, but that all the rest was as different as possible. For instance, the pictures on the wall next the fire seemed to be all alive, and the very clock on the chimney-piece (you know you can only see the back of it in the Looking-glass) had got the face of a little old man, and grinned at her.

'They don't keep this room so tidy as the other,' Alice thought to herself, as she noticed several of the chessmen down in the hearth among the cinders: but in another moment, with a little 'Oh!' of surprise, she was down on her hands and knees watching them. The chessmen were walking about, two and two!

'Here are the Red King and the Red Queen,' Alice said (in a whisper, for fear of frightening them), 'and there are the White King and the White Queen sitting on the edge of the shovel-and here are two castles walking arm in arm—I don't think they can hear me,' she went on, as she put her head closer down, 'and I'm nearly sure they can't see me. I feel somehow as if I were invisible—'

Here something began squeaking on the table behind Alice, and made her turn her head just in time to see one of the White Pawns roll over and begin kicking: she watched it with great curiosity to see what would happen next.

'It is the voice of my child!' the White Queen cried out as she rushed past the King, so violently that she knocked him over among the cinders. 'My precious Lily! My imperial kitten!' and she began scrambling wildly up the side of the fender.

'Imperial fiddlestick!' said the King, rubbing his nose, which had been hurt by the fall. He had a right to be a LITTLE annoyed with the Queen, for he was covered with ashes from head to foot.

Alice was very anxious to be of use, and, as the poor little Lily was nearly screaming herself into a fit, she hastily picked up the Queen and set her on the table by the side of her noisy little daughter.

The Queen gasped, and sat down: the rapid journey through the air had quite taken away her breath and for a minute or two she could do nothing but hug the little Lily in silence. As soon as she had recovered her breath a little, she called out to the White King, who was sitting sulkily among the ashes, 'Mind the volcano!'

'What volcano?' said the King, looking up anxiously into the fire, as if he thought that was the most likely place to find one.

'Blew—me—up,' panted the Queen, who was still a little out of breath. 'Mind you come up—the regular way—don't get blown up!'

Alice watched the White King as he slowly struggled up from bar to bar, till at last she said, 'Why, you'll be hours and hours getting to the table, at that rate. I'd far better help you, hadn't I?'

But the King took no notice of the question: it was quite clear that he could neither hear her nor see her.

So Alice picked him up very gently, and lifted him across more slowly than she had lifted the Queen, that she mightn't take his breath away: but, before she put him on the table, she thought she might as well dust him a little, he was so covered with ashes.

She said afterwards that she had never seen in all her life such a face as the King made, when he found himself held in the air by an invisible hand, and being dusted: he was far too much astonished to cry out, but his eyes and his mouth went on getting larger and larger, and rounder and rounder, till her hand shook so with laughing that she nearly let him drop upon the floor.

'Oh! PLEASE don't make such faces, my dear!' she cried out, quite forgetting that the King couldn't hear her. 'You make me laugh so that I can hardly hold you! And don't keep your mouth so wide open! All the ashes will get into it—there, now I think you're tidy enough!' she added, as she smoothed his hair, and set him upon the table near the Queen.

The King immediately fell flat on his back, and lay perfectly still: and Alice was a little alarmed at what she had done, and went round the room to see if she could find any water to throw over him. However, she could find nothing but a bottle of ink, and when she got back with it she found he had recovered, and he and the Queen were talking together in a frightened whisper—so low, that Alice could hardly hear what they said.

The King was saying, 'I assure, you my dear, I turned cold to the very ends of my whiskers!'

To which the Queen replied, 'You haven't got any whiskers.'

'The horror of that moment,' the King went on, 'I shall never, NEVER forget!'

'You will, though,' the Queen said, 'If you don't make a memorandum of it.'

Alice looked on with great interest as the King took an enormous memorandum-book out of his pocket, and began writing. A sudden thought struck her, and she took hold of the end of the pencil, which came some way over his shoulder, and began writing for him.

The poor King looked puzzled and unhappy, and struggled with the pencil for some time without saying anything; but Alice was too strong for him, and at last he panted out, 'My dear! I really MUST get a thinner pencil. I can't manage this one a bit; it writes all manner of things that I don't intend—'

'What manner of things?' said the Queen, looking over the book (in which Alice had put 'THE WHITE KNIGHT IS SLIDING DOWN THE POKER. HE BALANCES VERY BADLY') 'That's not a memorandum of YOUR feelings!'

There was a book lying near Alice on the table, and while she sat watching the White King (for she was still a little anxious about him, and had the ink all ready to throw over him, in case he fainted again), she turned over the leaves, to find some part that she could read, '—for it's all in some language I don't know,' she said to herself.

It was like this.

# YKCOWREBBAJ

sevot yhtils eht dna,gillirb sawT"

ebaw eht ni elbmig dna eryg diD

,sevogorob eht erew ysmim llA

.ebargtuo shtar emom eht dnA


She puzzled over this for some time, but at last
어리둥절하게[이해할 수 없게] 만들다
a bright thought struck her. 'Why, it's a Looking-
좋은 생각이 떠오르다
glass book, of course! And if I hold it up to a glass,
위로 펴다
the words will all go the right way again.'
글이 제대로 보이다
This was the poem that Alice read.
(한 편의) 시(詩)    읽다


## JABBERWOCKY
재버워크(무의미한 말[글], 알아들을 수 없는 말[글])

'Twas brillig, and the slithy toves
오후 4시          나긋하고 부지런한 토우브들은
Did gyre and gimble in the wabe;
땅을 파헤치며 구멍을 뚫다   언덕 가장자리에서
All mimsy were the borogoves,
불안한 버로고우브들과
And the mome raths outgrabe.
집나온 녹색 돼지들은 콧소리 내며 끽끽거렸네


'Beware the Jabberwock, my son!
조심[주의]하다
The jaws that bite, the claws that catch!
이빨로 물다       발톱으로 나꿔채다
Beware the Jubjub bird, and shun
주브주브 새          피하다

The frumious Bandersnatch!'
무섭고 오싹한 밴더 스내치

He took his vorpal sword in hand:
풀을 쳐서 베는 검
Long time the manxome foe he sought—
오랫동안 사람을 죽이는 괴물을 찾아다니다
So rested he by the Tumtum tree,
쉬다, 휴식하다    둥둥 나무 옆에서
And stood awhile in thought.
생각에 잠겨 잠시 서 있다

And as in uffish thought he stood,
몹시 거친 생각에 잠겨
The Jabberwock, with eyes of flame,
불꽃같은 눈의
Came whiffling through the tulgey wood,
바람을 가르고 튀어나오다    어둑하고 기괴한 숲 사이로
And burbled as it came!
부글부글 무서운 소리가 들리다

One, two! One, two! And through and through
찌르고, 또 찌르고
The vorpal blade went snicker-snack!
풀 베는 검                    날쌔게 날아다니다
He left it dead, and with its head
괴물을 죽이다        머리를 자르다
He went galumphing back.
의기양양하게 말을 타고 돌아오다

'And hast thou slain the Jabberwock?
(전쟁, 싸움에서) 죽이다; 살해하다
Come to my arms, my beamish boy!
자랑스러운; 빛나는; 기쁨에 넘친
O frabjous day! Callooh! Callay!'
멋진, 즐거운; 경사스러운    야호!
He chortled in his joy.
(기쁘거나 재미있어서) 깔깔거리다

'Twas brillig, and the slithy toves
오후의 끝자락

Did gyre and gimble in the wabe;
All mimsy were the borogoves,
And the mome raths outgrabe.

'It seems very pretty,' she said when she had finished it, 'but it's RATHER hard to understand!' (You see she didn't like to confess, even to herself, that she couldn't make it out at all.) 'Somehow it seems to fill my head with ideas—only I don't exactly know what they are! However, SOMEBODY killed SOMETHING: that's clear, at any rate—'

'But oh!' thought Alice, suddenly jumping up, 'If I don't make haste I shall have to go back through the Looking-glass, before I've seen what the rest of the house is like! Let's have a look at the garden first!' She was out of the room in a moment, and ran down stairs—or, at least, it wasn't exactly running, but a new invention of hers for getting down stairs quickly and easily, as Alice said to herself. She just kept the tips of her fingers on the hand-rail, and floated gently down without even touching the stairs with her feet; then she floated on through the hall, and would have gone straight out at the door in the same way, if she hadn't caught hold of the door-post. She was getting a little giddy with so much floating in the air, and was rather glad to find herself walking again in the natural way.

# CHAPTER II
# The Garden of Live Flowers

'I should see the garden far better,' said Alice to herself, 'If I could get to the top of that hill: and here's a path that leads straight to it—at least, no, it doesn't do that—' (after going a few yards along the path, and turning several sharp corners), 'but I suppose it will at last. But how curiously it twists! It's more like a corkscrew than a path! Well, THIS turn goes to the hill, I suppose—no, it doesn't! This goes straight back to the house! Well then, I'll try it the other way.'

And so she did: wandering up and down, and trying turn after turn, but always coming back to the house, do what she would. Indeed, once, when she turned a corner rather more quickly than usual, she ran against it before she could stop herself.

'It's no use talking about it,' Alice said, looking up at the house and pretending it was arguing with her. 'I'm NOT going in again yet. I know I should have to get through the Looking-glass again—back into the old room—and there'd be an end of all my adventures!'

So, resolutely turning her back upon the house, she set out once more down the path, determined to keep straight on till she got to the hill. For a few minutes all went on well, and she was just saying, 'I really SHALL do it this time—'d'd when the path gave a sudden twist and shook itself (as she described it afterwards), and the next moment she found herself actually walking in at the door.

'Oh, it's too bad!' she cried. 'I never saw such a house for getting in the way! Never!'

However, there was the hill full in sight, so there was nothing to be done but start again. This time she came upon a large flower-bed, with a border of daisies, and a willow-tree growing in the middle.

'O Tiger-lily,' said Alice, addressing herself to one that was waving gracefully about in the wind, 'I WISH you could talk!'

'We CAN talk,' said the Tiger-lily: 'when there's anybody worth talking to.'

Alice was so astonished that she could not

speak for a minute: it quite seemed to take her breath away. At length, as the Tiger-lily only went on waving about, she spoke again, in a timid voice—almost in a whisper. 'And can ALL the flowers talk?'

'As well as YOU can,' said the Tiger-lily. 'And a great deal louder.'

'It isn't manners for us to begin, you know,' said the Rose, 'and I really was wondering when you'd speak! Said I to myself, "Her face has got SOME sense in it, though it's not a clever one!" Still, you're the right colour, and that goes a long way.'

'I don't care about the colour,' the Tiger-lily remarked. 'If only her petals curled up a little more, she'd be all right.'

Alice didn't like being criticised, so she began asking questions. 'Aren't you sometimes frightened at being planted out here, with nobody to take care of you?'

'There's the tree in the middle,' said the Rose: 'what else is it good for?'

'But what could it do, if any danger came?' Alice asked.

'It says "Bough-wough!"' cried a Daisy: 'that's why its branches are called boughs!'

'didn't you know THAT?' cried another Daisy, and here they all began shouting together, till the air seemed quite full of little shrill voices. 'Silence, every one of you!' cried the Tiger-lily, waving itself passionately from side to side, and trembling with excitement. 'They know I can't get at them!' it panted, bending its quivering head towards Alice, 'or they wouldn't dare to do it!'

'Never mind!' Alice said in a soothing tone, and stooping down to the daisies, who were just beginning again, she whispered, 'If you don't hold your tongues, I'll pick you!'

There was silence in a moment, and several of the pink daisies turned white.

'That's right!' said the Tiger-lily. 'The daisies are worst of all. When one speaks, they all begin together, and it's enough to make one wither to hear the way they go on!'

'How is it you can all talk so nicely?' Alice said, hoping to get it into a better temper by a compliment. 'I've been in many gardens before, but none of the flowers could talk.'

'Put your hand down, and feel the ground,' said the Tiger-lily. 'Then you'll know why.'

Alice did so. 'It's very hard,' she said, 'but I don't see what that has to do with it.'

'In most gardens,' the Tiger-lily said, 'they make the beds too soft—so that the flowers are always asleep.'

This sounded a very good reason, and Alice was quite pleased to know it. 'I never thought of that before!' she said.

'It's MY opinion that you never think AT ALL,' the Rose said in a rather severe tone.

'I never saw anybody that looked stupider,' a Violet said, so suddenly, that Alice quite jumped; for it hadn't spoken before.

'Hold YOUR tongue!' cried the Tiger-lily. 'As if YOU ever saw anybody! You keep your head under the leaves, and snore away there, till you know no more what's going on in the world, than if you were a bud!'

'Are there any more people in the garden besides me?' Alice said, not choosing to notice the Rose's last remark.

'There's one other flower in the garden that can move about like you,' said the Rose. 'I wonder how you do it—' ('You're always wondering,' said the Tiger-lily), 'but she's more bushy than you are.'

'Is she like me?' Alice asked eagerly, for the thought crossed her mind, 'There's another little girl in the garden, somewhere!'

'Well, she has the same awkward shape as you,' the Rose said, 'but she's redder—and her petals are shorter, I think.'

'Her petals are done up close, almost like a dahlia,' the Tiger-lily interrupted: 'not tumbled about anyhow, like yours.'

'But that's not YOUR fault,' the Rose added kindly: 'you're beginning to fade, you know—and then one can't help one's petals getting a little untidy.'

Alice didn't like this idea at all: so, to change the subject, she asked 'Does she ever come out here?'

'I daresay you'll see her soon,' said the Rose. 'She's one of the thorny kind.'

'Where does she wear the thorns?' Alice asked with some curiosity.

'Why all round her head, of course,' the Rose replied. 'I was wondering YOU hadn't got some too. I thought it was the regular rule.'

'She's coming!' cried the Larkspur. 'I hear her footstep, thump, thump, thump, along the gravel-walk!'

Alice looked round eagerly, and found that it was the Red Queen. 'She's grown a good deal!' was her first remark. She had indeed: when Alice first found her in the ashes, she had been only three inches high—and here she was, half a head taller than Alice herself!

'It's the fresh air that does it,' said the Rose: 'wonderfully fine air it is, out here.'

'I think I'll go and meet her,' said Alice, for, though the flowers were interesting enough, she felt that it would be far grander to have a talk with a real Queen.

'You can't possibly do that,' said the Rose: 'I

should advise you to walk the other way.'
This sounded nonsense to Alice, so she said nothing, but set off at once towards the Red Queen. To her surprise, she lost sight of her in a moment, and found herself walking in at the front-door again.

A little provoked, she drew back, and after looking everywhere for the queen (whom she spied out at last, a long way off), she thought she would try the plan, this time, of walking in the opposite direction.

It succeeded beautifully. She had not been walking a minute before she found herself face to face with the Red Queen, and full in sight of the hill she had been so long aiming at.

'Where do you come from?' said the Red Queen. 'And where are you going? Look up, speak nicely, and don't twiddle your fingers all the time.'

Alice attended to all these directions, and explained, as well as she could, that she had lost her way.

'I don't know what you mean by YOUR way,' said the Queen: 'all the ways about here belong to ME—but why did you come out here at all?' she added in a kinder tone. 'Curtsey while you're thinking what to say, it saves time.'

Alice wondered a little at this, but she was too much in awe of the Queen to disbelieve it. 'I'll try it when I go home,' she thought to herself, 'the next time I'm a little late for dinner.'

'It's time for you to answer now,' the Queen said, looking at her watch: 'open your mouth a LITTLE wider when you speak, and always say "your Majesty."'

'I only wanted to see what the garden was like, your Majesty—'

'That's right,' said the Queen, patting her on the head, which Alice didn't like at all, 'though, when you say "garden,"—I'VE seen gardens, compared with which this would be a wilderness.'

Alice didn't dare to argue the point, but went on: '—and I thought I'd try and find my way to the top of that hill—'

'When you say "hill,"' the Queen interrupted, '*I* could show you hills, in comparison with which you'd call that a valley.'

'No, I shouldn't,' said Alice, surprised into contradicting her at last: 'a hill CAN'T be a valley, you know. That would be nonsense—'

The Red Queen shook her head, 'You may call it "nonsense" if you like,' she said, 'but I'VE heard nonsense, compared with which that would be as sensible as a dictionary!'

Alice curtseyed again, as she was afraid from the Queen's tone that she was a LITTLE offended: and they walked on in silence till they got to the top of the little hill.

For some minutes Alice stood without speaking, looking out in all directions over the country—and a most curious country it was. There were a number of tiny little brooks running straight across it from side to side, and the ground between was divided up into squares by a number of little green hedges, that reached from brook to brook.

'I declare it's marked out just like a large chess-board!' Alice said at last. 'There ought to be some men moving about somewhere—and so there are!' She added in a tone of delight, and her heart began to beat quick with excitement as she went on. 'It's a great huge game of chess that's being played—all over the world—if this IS the world at all, you know. Oh, what fun it is! How I WISH I was one of them! I wouldn't mind being a Pawn, if only I might join—though of course I should LIKE to be a Queen, best.'

She glanced rather shyly at the real Queen as she said this, but her companion only smiled pleasantly, and said, 'That's easily managed. You can be the White Queen's Pawn, if you like, as Lily's too young to play; and you're in the Second Square to begin with: when you get to the Eighth Square you'll be a Queen—' Just at this moment, somehow or other, they began to run.

Alice never could quite make out, in thinking it over afterwards, how it was that they began: all she remembers is, that they were running hand in hand, and the Queen went so fast that it was all she could do to keep up with her: and still the Queen kept crying 'Faster! Faster!' but Alice felt she COULD NOT go faster, though she had not breath left to say so.

The most curious part of the thing was, that the trees and the other things round them never changed their places at all: however fast they went, they never seemed to pass anything. 'I wonder if all the things move along with us?' thought poor puzzled Alice. And the Queen seemed to guess her thoughts, for she cried, 'Faster! Don't try to talk!'

Not that Alice had any idea of doing THAT. She felt as if she would never be able to talk again, she was getting so much out of breath: and still the Queen cried 'Faster! Faster!' and dragged her along. 'Are we nearly there?' Alice managed to pant out at last.

'Nearly there!' the Queen repeated. 'Why, we passed it ten minutes ago! Faster!' And they ran on for a time in silence, with the wind whistling in Alice's ears, and almost blowing her hair off her head, she fancied.

'Now! Now!' cried the Queen. 'Faster! Faster!' And they went so fast that at last they seemed to skim through the air, hardly touching the ground with their feet, till suddenly, just as Alice was getting quite exhausted, they stopped, and she found herself sitting on the ground, breathless and giddy.

The Queen propped her up against a tree, and said kindly, 'You may rest a little now.'

Alice looked round her in great surprise. 'Why, I do believe we've been under this tree the whole time! Everything's just as it was!'

'Of course it is,' said the Queen, 'what would you have it?'

'Well, in OUR country,' said Alice, still panting a little, 'you'd generally get to somewhere else—if you ran very fast for a long time, as we've been doing.'

'A slow sort of country!' said the Queen. 'Now, HERE, you see, it takes all the running YOU can do, to keep in the same place. If you want to get somewhere else, you must run at least twice as fast as that!'

'I'd rather not try, please!' said Alice. 'I'm quite content to stay here—only I AM so hot and thirsty!'

'I know what YOU'd like!' the Queen said

good-naturedly, taking a little box out of her pocket. 'Have a biscuit?'

Alice thought it would not be civil to say 'No,' though it wasn't at all what she wanted. So she took it, and ate it as well as she could: and it was VERY dry; and she thought she had never been so nearly choked in all her life.

'While you're refreshing yourself,' said the Queen, 'I'll just take the measurements.' And she took a ribbon out of her pocket, marked in inches, and began measuring the ground, and sticking little pegs in here and there.

'At the end of two yards,' she said, putting in a peg to mark the distance, 'I shall give you your directions—have another biscuit?'

'No, thank you,' said Alice: 'one's QUITE enough!'

'Thirst quenched, I hope?' said the Queen.

Alice did not know what to say to this, but luckily the Queen did not wait for an answer, but went on. 'At the end of THREE yards I shall repeat them—for fear of your forgetting them. At the end of FOUR, I shall say good-bye. And at the end of FIVE, I shall go!'

She had got all the pegs put in by this time, and Alice looked on with great interest as she returned to the tree, and then began slowly walking down the row.

At the two-yard peg she faced round, and said, 'A pawn goes two squares in its first move, you know. So you'll go VERY quickly through the Third Square—by railway, I should think—and you'll find yourself in the Fourth Square in no time. Well, THAT square belongs to Tweedledum and Tweedledee—the Fifth is mostly water—the Sixth belongs to Humpty Dumpty—But you make no remark?'

'I—I didn't know I had to make one—just then,' Alice faltered out.

'You SHOULD have said, "It's extremely kind of you to tell me all this"—however, we'll suppose it said—the Seventh Square is all forest—however, one of the Knights will show you the way—and in the Eighth Square we shall be Queens together, and it's all feasting and fun!' Alice got up and curtseyed, and sat down again.

At the next peg the Queen turned again, and this time she said, 'Speak in French when you can't think of the English for a thing—turn out your toes as you walk—and remember who you are!' She did not wait for Alice to curtsey this time, but walked on quickly to the next peg, where she turned for a moment to say 'good-bye,' and then hurried on to the last.

How it happened, Alice never knew, but exactly as she came to the last peg, she was gone. Whether she vanished into the air, or whether she ran quickly into the wood ('and she CAN run very fast!' thought Alice), there was no way of guessing, but she was gone, and Alice began to remember that she was a Pawn, and that it would soon be time for her to move.

# CHAPTER III

## Looking-Glass Insects

Of course the first thing to do was to make a grand survey of the country she was going to travel through. 'It's something very like learning geography,' thought Alice, as she stood on tiptoe in hopes of being able to see a little further. 'Principal rivers—there ARE none. Principal mountains—I'm on the only one, but I don't think it's got any name. Principal towns—why, what ARE those creatures, making honey down there? They can't be bees—nobody ever saw bees a mile off, you know—' and for some time she stood silent, watching one of them that was bustling about among the flowers, poking its proboscis into them, 'just as if it was a regular bee,' thought Alice.

However, this was anything but a regular bee: in fact it was an elephant—as Alice soon found out, though the idea quite took her breath away at first. 'And what enormous flowers they must be!'

was her next idea. 'Something like cottages with the roofs taken off, and stalks put to them—and what quantities of honey they must make! I think I'll go down and—no, I won't JUST yet,' she went on, checking herself just as she was beginning to run down the hill, and trying to find some excuse for turning shy so suddenly. 'It'll never do to go down among them without a good long branch to brush them away—and what fun it'll be when they ask me how I like my walk. I shall say—"Oh, I like it well enough—"' (here came the favourite little toss of the head), '"only it was so dusty and hot, and the elephants did tease so!"'

'I think I'll go down the other way,' she said after a pause: 'and perhaps I may visit the elephants later on. Besides, I do so want to get into the Third Square!'

So with this excuse she ran down the hill and jumped over the first of the six little brooks.

\*   \*   \*   \*   \*   \*   \*

\*   \*   \*   \*   \*   \*

\*   \*   \*   \*   \*   \*   \*

'Tickets, please!' said the Guard, putting his

head in at the window. In a moment everybody was holding out a ticket: they were about the same size as the people, and quite seemed to fill the carriage.

'Now then! Show your ticket, child!' the Guard went on, looking angrily at Alice. And a great many voices all said together ('like the chorus of a song,' thought Alice), 'Don't keep him waiting, child! Why, his time is worth a thousand pounds a minute!'

'I'm afraid I haven't got one,' Alice said in a frightened tone: 'There wasn't a ticket-office where I came from.' And again the chorus of voices went on. 'There wasn't room for one where she came from. The land there is worth a thousand pounds an inch!'

'Don't make excuses,' said the Guard: 'you should have bought one from the engine-driver.' And once more the chorus of voices went on with 'The man that drives the engine. Why, the smoke alone is worth a thousand pounds a puff!'

Alice thought to herself, 'Then there's no use in speaking.' The voices didn't join in this time, as she hadn't spoken, but to her great surprise, they all THOUGHT in chorus (I hope you understand what THINKING IN CHORUS means—for I must confess that *I* don't), 'Better say nothing at all. Language is worth a thousand pounds a word!'

'I shall dream about a thousand pounds to-night, I know I shall!' thought Alice.

All this time the Guard was looking at her, first through a telescope, then through a microscope, and then through an opera-glass. At last he said, 'You're travelling the wrong way,' and shut up the window and went away.

'So young a child,' said the gentleman sitting opposite to her (he was dressed in white paper), 'ought to know which way she's going, even if she doesn't know her own name!'

A Goat, that was sitting next to the gentleman in white, shut his eyes and said in a loud voice, 'She ought to know her way to the ticket-office, even if she doesn't know her alphabet!'

There was a Beetle sitting next to the Goat (it was a very queer carriage-full of passengers altogether), and, as the rule seemed to be that they should all speak in turn, HE went on with 'She'll have to go back from here as luggage!'

Alice couldn't see who was sitting beyond the Beetle, but a hoarse voice spoke next. 'Change engines—' it said, and was obliged to leave off.

'It sounds like a horse,' Alice thought to herself. And an extremely small voice, close to her ear, said, 'You might make a joke on that—something about "horse" and "hoarse," you know.'

Then a very gentle voice in the distance said, 'She must be labelled "Lass, with care," you know—'

And after that other voices went on ('What a number of people there are in the carriage!' thought Alice), saying, 'She must go by post, as she's got a head on her—' 'She must be sent as a message by the telegraph—' 'She must draw the train herself the rest of the way—' and so on.

But the gentleman dressed in white paper leaned forwards and whispered in her ear, 'Never mind what they all say, my dear, but take a return-ticket every time the train stops.'

'Indeed I shan't!' Alice said rather impatiently.

'I don't belong to this railway journey at all—I was in a wood just now—and I wish I could get back there.'

'You might make a joke on THAT said the little voice close to her ear: 'something about "you WOULD if you could," you know.'

'Don't tease so,' said Alice, looking about in vain to see where the voice came from; 'If you're so anxious to have a joke made, why don't you make one yourself?'

The little voice sighed deeply: it was VERY unhappy, evidently, and Alice would have said something pitying to comfort it, 'If it would only sigh like other people!' she thought. But this was such a wonderfully small sigh, that she wouldn't have heard it at all, if it hadn't come QUITE close to her ear. The consequence of this was that it tickled her ear very much, and quite took off her thoughts from the unhappiness of the poor little creature.

'I know you are a friend,' the little voice went on; 'a dear friend, and an old friend. And you won't hurt me, though I AM an insect.'

'What kind of insect?' Alice inquired a little anxiously. What she really wanted to know was, whether it could sting or not, but she thought this wouldn't be quite a civil question to ask.

'What, then you don't—' the little voice began, when it was drowned by a shrill scream from the engine, and everybody jumped up in alarm, Alice among the rest.

The Horse, who had put his head out of the window, quietly drew it in and said, 'It's only a brook we have to jump over.' Everybody seemed satisfied with this, though Alice felt a little nervous at the idea of trains jumping at all. 'However, it'll take us into the Fourth Square, that's some comfort!' she said to herself. In another moment she felt the carriage rise straight up into the air, and in her fright she caught at the thing nearest to her hand, which happened to be the Goat's beard.

\* \* \* \* \* \* \*

\* \* \* \* \* \*

\* \* \* \* \* \* \*

But the beard seemed to melt away as she touched it, and she found herself sitting quietly under a tree—while the Gnat (for that was the insect she had been talking to) was balancing itself on a twig just over her head, and fanning her with its wings.

It certainly was a VERY large Gnat: 'about the size of a chicken,' Alice thought. Still, she couldn't feel nervous with it, after they had been talking together so long.

'—then you don't like all insects?' the Gnat went on, as quietly as if nothing had happened.

'I like them when they can talk,' Alice said. 'None of them ever talk, where *I* come from.'

'What sort of insects do you rejoice in, where YOU come from?' the Gnat inquired.

'I don't REJOICE in insects at all,' Alice explained, 'because I'm rather afraid of them—at least the large kinds. But I can tell you the names of some of them.'

'Of course they answer to their names?' the Gnat remarked carelessly.

'I never knew them to do it.'

'What's the use of their having names,' the Gnat said, 'If they won't answer to them?'

'No use to THEM,' said Alice; 'but it's useful to the people who name them, I suppose. If not, why do things have names at all?'

'I can't say,' the Gnat replied. 'Further on, in the wood down there, they've got no names—however, go on with your list of insects: you're wasting time.'

'Well, there's the Horse-fly,' Alice began, counting off the names on her fingers.

'All right,' said the Gnat: 'half way up that bush, you'll see a Rocking-horse-fly, if you look. It's made entirely of wood, and gets about by swinging itself from branch to branch.'

'What does it live on?' Alice asked, with great curiosity.

'Sap and sawdust,' said the Gnat. 'Go on with the list.'

Alice looked up at the Rocking-horse-fly with great interest, and made up her mind that it must have been just repainted, it looked so bright and sticky; and then she went on.

'And there's the Dragon-fly.'

'Look on the branch above your head,' said

the Gnat, 'and there you'll find a snap-dragon-fly. Its body is made of plum-pudding, its wings of holly-leaves, and its head is a raisin burning in brandy.'

'And what does it live on?'

'Frumenty and mince pie,' the Gnat replied; 'and it makes its nest in a Christmas box.'

'And then there's the Butterfly,' Alice went on, after she had taken a good look at the insect with its head on fire, and had thought to herself, 'I wonder if that's the reason insects are so fond of flying into candles—because they want to turn into Snap-dragon-flies!'

'Crawling at your feet,' said the Gnat (Alice drew her feet back in some alarm), 'you may observe a Bread-and-Butterfly. Its wings are thin slices of Bread-and-butter, its body is a crust, and its head is a lump of sugar.'

'And what does IT live on?'

'Weak tea with cream in it.'

A new difficulty came into Alice's head. 'Supposing it couldn't find any?' she suggested.

'Then it would die, of course.'

'But that must happen very often,' Alice remarked thoughtfully.

'It always happens,' said the Gnat.

After this, Alice was silent for a minute or two, pondering. The Gnat amused itself meanwhile by humming round and round her head: at last it settled again and remarked, 'I suppose you don't want to lose your name?'

'No, indeed,' Alice said, a little anxiously.

'And yet I don't know,' the Gnat went on in a careless tone: 'only think how convenient it would be if you could manage to go home without it! For instance, if the governess wanted to call you to your lessons, she would call out "come here—," and there she would have to leave off, because there wouldn't be any name for her to call, and of course you wouldn't have to go, you know.'

'That would never do, I'm sure,' said Alice: 'The governess would never think of excusing me lessons for that. If she couldn't remember my name, she'd call me "Miss!" as the servants do.'

'Well, if she said "Miss," and didn't say anything more,' the Gnat remarked, 'of course you'd miss your lessons. That's a joke. I wish YOU had made it.'

'Why do you wish *I* had made it?' Alice asked.

'It's a very bad one.'

But the Gnat only sighed deeply, while two large tears came rolling down its cheeks.

'You shouldn't make jokes,' Alice said, 'If it makes you so unhappy.'

Then came another of those melancholy little sighs, and this time the poor Gnat really seemed to have sighed itself away, for, when Alice looked up, there was nothing whatever to be seen on the twig, and, as she was getting quite chilly with sitting still so long, she got up and walked on.

She very soon came to an open field, with a wood on the other side of it: it looked much darker than the last wood, and Alice felt a LITTLE timid about going into it. However, on second thoughts, she made up her mind to go on: 'for I certainly won't go BACK,' she thought to herself, and this was the only way to the Eighth Square.

'This must be the wood,' she said thoughtfully to herself, 'where things have no names. I wonder what'll become of MY name when I go in? I shouldn't like to lose it at all—because they'd have to give me another, and it would be almost certain to be an ugly one. But then the fun would be trying to find the creature that had got my old name! That's just like the advertisements, you know, when people lose dogs—"ANSWERS TO THE NAME OF 'DASH:' HAD ON A BRASS COLLAR"—just fancy calling everything you met "Alice," till one of them answered! Only they wouldn't answer at all, if they were wise.'

She was rambling on in this way when she reached the wood: it looked very cool and shady. 'Well, at any rate it's a great comfort,' she said as she stepped under the trees, 'after being so hot, to get into the—into WHAT?' she went on, rather surprised at not being able to think of the word. 'I mean to get under the—under the—under THIS, you know!' putting her hand on the trunk of the tree. 'What DOES it call itself, I wonder? I do believe it's got no name—why, to be sure it hasn't!'

She stood silent for a minute, thinking: then she suddenly began again. 'Then it really HAS happened, after all! And now, who am I? I WILL remember, if I can! I'm determined to do it!' But being determined didn't help much, and all she could say, after a great deal of puzzling, was, 'L, I KNOW it begins with L!'

Just then a Fawn came wandering by: it looked at Alice with its large gentle eyes, but didn't seem at all frightened. 'Here then! Here then!' Alice said, as she held out her hand and tried to stroke it; but it only started back a little, and then stood looking at her again.

'What do you call yourself?' the Fawn said at last. Such a soft sweet voice it had!

'I wish I knew!' thought poor Alice. She answered, rather sadly, 'Nothing, just now.'

'Think again,' it said: 'that won't do.'

Alice thought, but nothing came of it. 'Please, would you tell me what YOU call yourself?' she said timidly. 'I think that might help a little.'

'I'll tell you, if you'll move a little further on,' the Fawn said. 'I can't remember here.'

So they walked on together through the wood, Alice with her arms clasped lovingly round the soft neck of the Fawn, till they came out into another open field, and here the Fawn gave a sudden bound into the air, and shook itself free from Alice's arms. 'I'm a Fawn!' it cried out in a voice of delight, 'and, dear me! you're a human child!' A sudden look of alarm came into its beautiful brown eyes, and in another moment it had darted away at full speed.

Alice stood looking after it, almost ready to cry with vexation at having lost her dear little fellow-traveller so suddenly. 'However, I know my name now.' she said, 'that's SOME comfort. Alice-Alice—I won't forget it again. And now, which of these finger-posts ought I to follow, I wonder?'

It was not a very difficult question to answer, as there was only one road through the wood, and the two finger-posts both pointed along it. 'I'll settle it,' Alice said to herself, 'when the road divides and they point different ways.'

But this did not seem likely to happen. She went on and on, a long way, but wherever the road divided there were sure to be two finger-posts pointing the same way, one marked 'TO

TWEEDLEDUM'S HOUSE' and the other 'TO THE HOUSE OF TWEEDLEDEE.'

'I do believe,' said Alice at last, 'that they live in the same house! I wonder I never thought of that before—But I can't stay there long. I'll just call and say "how d'you do?" and ask them the way out of the wood. If I could only get to the Eighth Square before it gets dark!' So she wandered on, talking to herself as she went, till, on turning a sharp corner, she came upon two fat little men, so suddenly that she could not help starting back, but in another moment she recovered herself, feeling sure that they must be.

# CHAPTER IV
# Tweedledum And Tweedledee

They were standing under a tree, each with an arm round the other's neck, and Alice knew which was which in a moment, because one of them had 'DUM' embroidered on his collar, and the other 'DEE.' 'I suppose they've each got "TWEEDLE" round at the back of the collar,' she said to herself.

They stood so still that she quite forgot they were alive, and she was just looking round to see if the word "TWEEDLE" was written at the back of each collar, when she was startled by a voice coming from the one marked 'DUM.'

'If you think we're wax-works,' he said, 'you ought to pay, you know. Wax-works weren't made to be looked at for nothing, nohow!'

'Contrariwise,' added the one marked 'DEE,' 'If you think we're alive, you ought to speak.'

'I'm sure I'm very sorry,' was all Alice could say; for the words of the old song kept ringing through her head like the ticking of a clock, and she could hardly help saying them out loud:—

'Tweedledum and Tweedledee
　Agreed to have a battle;
For Tweedledum said Tweedledee
　Had spoiled his nice new rattle.

Just then flew down a monstrous crow,
　As black as a tar-barrel;
Which frightened both the heroes so,
　They quite forgot their quarrel.'

'I know what you're thinking about,' said Tweedledum: 'but it isn't so, nohow.'

'Contrariwise,' continued Tweedledee, 'If it was so, it might be; and if it were so, it would be; but as it isn't, it ain't. That's logic.'

'I was thinking,' Alice said very politely, 'which is the best way out of this wood: it's getting so dark. Would you tell me, please?'

But the little men only looked at each other and grinned.

They looked so exactly like a couple of great schoolboys, that Alice couldn't help pointing her finger at Tweedledum, and saying 'First Boy!'

'Nohow!' Tweedledum cried out briskly, and shut his mouth up again with a snap.

'Next Boy!' said Alice, passing on to Tweedledee, though she felt quite certain he would only shout out 'Contrariwise!' and so he did.

'You've been wrong!' cried Tweedledum. 'The first thing in a visit is to say "How d'ye do?" and shake hands!' And here the two brothers gave each other a hug, and then they held out the two hands that were free, to shake hands with her.

Alice did not like shaking hands with either of them first, for fear of hurting the other one's feelings; so, as the best way out of the difficulty, she took hold of both hands at once: the next moment they were dancing round in a ring. This seemed quite natural (she remembered afterwards), and she was not even surprised to hear music playing: it seemed to come from the tree under which they were dancing, and it was done (as well as she could make it out) by the branches rubbing one across the other, like fiddles and fiddle-sticks.

'But it certainly WAS funny,' (Alice said afterwards, when she was telling her sister the history of all this,) ' to find myself singing "HERE WE GO ROUND THE MULBERRY BUSH." I don't know when I began it, but somehow I felt as if I'd been singing it a long long time!'

The other two dancers were fat, and very soon out of breath. 'Four times round is enough for one dance,' Tweedledum panted out, and they left off dancing as suddenly as they had begun: the music stopped at the same moment.

Then they let go of Alice's hands, and stood looking at her for a minute: there was a rather awkward pause, as Alice didn't know how to begin a conversation with people she had just been dancing with. 'It would never do to say "How d'ye do?" NOW,' she said to herself: 'we seem to have got beyond that, somehow!'

'I hope you're not much tired?' she said at last.

'Nohow. And thank you VERY much for asking,' said Tweedledum.

'So much obliged!' added Tweedledee. 'You like

poetry?'

'Ye-es, pretty well—SOME poetry,' Alice said doubtfully. 'Would you tell me which road leads out of the wood?'

'What shall I repeat to her?' said Tweedledee, looking round at Tweedledum with great solemn eyes, and not noticing Alice's question.

'"THE WALRUS AND THE CARPENTER" is the longest,' Tweedledum replied, giving his brother an affectionate hug.

Tweedledee began instantly:

'The sun was shining—'

Here Alice ventured to interrupt him. 'If it's VERY long,' she said, as politely as she could, 'would you please tell me first which road—'

Tweedledee smiled gently, and began again:

'The sun was shining on the sea,

　Shining with all his might:
He did his very best to make
　The billows smooth and bright—

And this was odd, because it was
The middle of the night.


The moon was shining sulkily,
Because she thought the sun
Had got no business to be there
After the day was done—
"It's very rude of him," she said,
"To come and spoil the fun!"


The sea was wet as wet could be,
The sands were dry as dry.
You could not see a cloud, because
No cloud was in the sky:
No birds were flying over head—
There were no birds to fly.


The Walrus and the Carpenter
Were walking close at hand;
They wept like anything to see
Such quantities of sand:
"If this were only cleared away,"
They said, "it WOULD be grand!"

"If seven maids with seven mops
Swept it for half a year,
Do you suppose," the Walrus said,

"That they could get it clear?"

"I doubt it," said the Carpenter,
And shed a bitter tear.


"O Oysters, come and walk with us!"
The Walrus did beseech.
"A pleasant walk, a pleasant talk,
Along the briny beach:
We cannot do with more than four,

To give a hand to each."


The eldest Oyster looked at him.
But never a word he said:
The eldest Oyster winked his eye,
And shook his heavy head—
Meaning to say he did not choose
To leave the oyster-bed.


But four young oysters hurried up,

All eager for the treat:
Their coats were brushed, their faces washed,
Their shoes were clean and neat—
And this was odd, because, you know,
They hadn't any feet.


Four other Oysters followed them,
And yet another four;
And thick and fast they came at last,
And more, and more, and more—
All hopping through the frothy waves,
And scrambling to the shore.


The Walrus and the Carpenter
Walked on a mile or so,
And then they rested on a rock
Conveniently low:
And all the little Oysters stood
And waited in a row.


"The time has come," the Walrus said,
"To talk of many things:
Of shoes—and ships—and sealing-wax—

Of cabbages—and kings—
And why the sea is boiling hot—
And whether pigs have wings."


"But wait a bit," the Oysters cried,
"Before we have our chat;
For some of us are out of breath,
And all of us are fat!"
"No hurry!" said the Carpenter.
They thanked him much for that.


"A loaf of bread," the Walrus said,
"Is what we chiefly need:
Pepper and vinegar besides
Are very good indeed—
Now if you're ready Oysters dear,
We can begin to feed."


"But not on us!" the Oysters cried,
Turning a little blue,
"After such kindness, that would be
A dismal thing to do!"
"The night is fine," the Walrus said

"Do you admire the view?

"It was so kind of you to come!

And you are very nice!"

The Carpenter said nothing but

"Cut us another slice:

I wish you were not quite so deaf—

I've had to ask you twice!"


"It seems a shame," the Walrus said,

"To play them such a trick,

After we've brought them out so far,

And made them trot so quick!"

The Carpenter said nothing but

"The butter's spread too thick!"


"I weep for you," the Walrus said.

"I deeply sympathize."

With sobs and tears he sorted out

Those of the largest size.

Holding his pocket handkerchief

Before his streaming eyes.

"O Oysters," said the Carpenter.

"You've had a pleasant run!

Shall we be trotting home again?"

But answer came there none—

And that was scarcely odd, because

They'd eaten every one.'


'I like the Walrus best,' said Alice: 'because you see he was a LITTLE sorry for the poor oysters.'

'He ate more than the Carpenter, though,' said Tweedledee. 'You see he held his handkerchief in front, so that the Carpenter couldn't count how many he took: contrariwise.'

'That was mean!' Alice said indignantly. 'Then I like the Carpenter best—if he didn't eat so many as the Walrus.'

'But he ate as many as he could get,' said Tweedledum.

This was a puzzler. After a pause, Alice began, 'Well! They were BOTH very unpleasant characters—' Here she checked herself in some alarm, at hearing something that sounded to her like the puffing of a large steam-engine in the wood near them, though she feared it was more likely to be a wild beast. 'Are there any lions or tigers about here?' she asked timidly.

'It's only the Red King snoring,' said Tweedledee.

'Come and look at him!' the brothers cried, and they each took one of Alice's hands, and led her up to where the King was sleeping.

'Isn't he a LOVELY sight?' said Tweedledum.

Alice couldn't say honestly that he was. He had a tall red night-cap on, with a tassel, and he was lying crumpled up into a sort of untidy heap, and snoring loud—'fit to snore his head off!' as Tweedledum remarked.

'I'm afraid he'll catch cold with lying on the damp grass,' said Alice, who was a very thoughtful little girl.

'He's dreaming now,' said Tweedledee: 'and what do you think he's dreaming about?'

Alice said 'Nobody can guess that.'

'Why, about YOU!' Tweedledee exclaimed, clapping his hands triumphantly. 'And if he left off dreaming about you, where do you suppose you'd be?'

'Where I am now, of course,' said Alice.

'Not you!' Tweedledee retorted contemptuously. 'You'd be nowhere. Why, you're only a sort of thing in his dream!'

'If that there King was to wake,' added Tweedledum, 'you'd go out—bang!—just like a candle!'

'I shouldn't!' Alice exclaimed indignantly. 'Besides, if I'm only a sort of thing in his dream, what are YOU, I should like to know?'

'ditto' said Tweedledum.

'ditto, ditto' cried Tweedledee.

He shouted this so loud that Alice couldn't help saying, 'Hush! You'll be waking him, I'm afraid, if you make so much noise.'

'Well, it no use YOUR talking about waking him,' said Tweedledum, 'when you're only one of the things in his dream. You know very well you're not real.'

'I AM real!' said Alice and began to cry.

'You won't make yourself a bit realler by crying,' Tweedledee remarked: 'there's nothing to cry about.'

'If I wasn't real,' Alice said—half-laughing through her tears, it all seemed so ridiculous—'I shouldn't be able to cry.'

'I hope you don't suppose those are real tears?' Tweedledum interrupted in a tone of great contempt.

'I know they're talking nonsense,' Alice thought to herself: 'and it's foolish to cry about it.' So she brushed away her tears, and went on as cheerfully as she could. 'At any rate I'd better be getting out of the wood, for really it's coming on very dark. Do you think it's going to rain?'

Tweedledum spread a large umbrella over himself and his brother, and looked up into it. 'No, I don't think it is,' he said: 'at least—not under HERE. Nohow.'

'But it may rain OUTSIDE?'

'It may—if it chooses,' said Tweedledee: 'we've no objection. Contrariwise.'

'Selfish things!' thought Alice, and she was just going to say 'Good-night' and leave them, when Tweedledum sprang out from under the umbrella and seized her by the wrist.

'Do you see THAT?' he said, in a voice choking with passion, and his eyes grew large and yellow all in a moment, as he pointed with a trembling finger at a small white thing lying under the tree.

'It's only a rattle,' Alice said, after a careful examination of the little white thing. 'Not a rattle-SNAKE, you know,' she added hastily, thinking that he was frightened: 'only an old rattle—quite old and broken.'

'I knew it was!' cried Tweedledum, beginning to stamp about wildly and tear his hair. 'It's spoilt, of course!' Here he looked at Tweedledee, who immediately sat down on the ground, and tried to hide himself under the umbrella.

Alice laid her hand upon his arm, and said in a soothing tone, 'You needn't be so angry about an old rattle.'

'But it isn't old!' Tweedledum cried, in a greater fury than ever. 'It's new, I tell you—I bought it yesterday—my nice new RATTLE!' and his voice rose to a perfect scream.

All this time Tweedledee was trying his best to fold up the umbrella, with himself in it: which was such an extraordinary thing to do, that it quite took off Alice's attention from the angry brother. But he couldn't quite succeed, and it ended in his rolling over, bundled up in the umbrella, with only his head out: and there he lay, opening and shutting his mouth and his large eyes—'looking more like a fish than anything else,' Alice thought.

'Of course you agree to have a battle?' Tweedledum said in a calmer tone.

'I suppose so,' the other sulkily replied, as he crawled out of the umbrella: 'only SHE must help us to dress up, you know.'

So the two brothers went off hand-in-hand into the wood, and returned in a minute with their arms full of things—such as bolsters, blankets, hearth-rugs, table-cloths, dish-covers and coal-scuttles. 'I hope you're a good hand at pinning and tying strings?' Tweedledum remarked. 'Every one of these things has got to go on, somehow or other.'

Alice said afterwards she had never seen such a fuss made about anything in all her life—the way those two bustled about—and the quantity of things they put on—and the trouble they gave her in tying strings and fastening buttons—'Really they'll be more like bundles of old clothes than anything else, by the time they're ready!' she said to herself, as she arranged a bolster round the neck of Tweedledee, 'to keep his head from being cut off,' as he said.

'You know,' he added very gravely, 'It's one of the most serious things that can possibly happen to one in a battle—to get one's head cut off.'

Alice laughed aloud: but she managed to turn it into a cough, for fear of hurting his feelings.

'Do I look very pale?' said Tweedledum, coming up to have his helmet tied on. (He CALLED it a helmet, though it certainly looked much more like a saucepan.)

'Well—yes—a LITTLE,' Alice replied gently.

'I'm very brave generally,' he went on in a low voice: 'only to-day I happen to have a headache.'

'And I'VE got a toothache!' said Tweedledee, who had overheard the remark. 'I'm far worse off than you!'

'Then you'd better not fight to-day,' said Alice,

thinking it a good opportunity to make peace.

'We MUST have a bit of a fight, but I don't care about going on long,' said Tweedledum. 'What's the time now?'

Tweedledee looked at his watch, and said 'Half-past four.'

'Let's fight till six, and then have dinner,' said Tweedledum.

'Very well,' the other said, rather sadly: 'and SHE can watch us—only you'd better not come VERY close,' he added: 'I generally hit everything I can see—when I get really excited.'

'And *I* hit everything within reach,' cried Tweedledum, 'whether I can see it or not!'

Alice laughed. 'You must hit the TREES pretty often, I should think,' she said.

Tweedledum looked round him with a satisfied smile. 'I don't suppose,' he said, 'there'll be a tree left standing, for ever so far round, by the time we've finished!'

'And all about a rattle!' said Alice, still hoping to make them a LITTLE ashamed of fighting for such a trifle.

'I shouldn't have minded it so much,' said Tweedledum, 'If it hadn't been a new one.'

'I wish the monstrous crow would come!' thought Alice.

'There's only one sword, you know,' Tweedledum said to his brother: 'but you can have the umbrella—it's quite as sharp. Only we must begin quick. It's getting as dark as it can.'

'And darker,' said Tweedledee.

It was getting dark so suddenly that Alice thought there must be a thunderstorm coming on. 'What a thick black cloud that is!' she said. 'And how fast it comes! Why, I do believe it's got wings!'

'It's the crow!' Tweedledum cried out in a shrill voice of alarm: and the two brothers took to their heels and were out of sight in a moment.

Alice ran a little way into the wood, and stopped under a large tree. 'It can never get at me HERE,' she thought: 'It's far too large to squeeze itself in among the trees. But I wish it wouldn't flap its wings so—it makes quite a hurricane in the wood—here's somebody's shawl being blown away!'

# CHAPTER V

# Wool and Water

She caught the shawl as she spoke, and looked about for the owner: in another moment the White Queen came running wildly through the wood, with both arms stretched out wide, as if she were flying, and Alice very civilly went to meet her with the shawl.

'I'm very glad I happened to be in the way,' Alice said, as she helped her to put on her shawl again.

The White Queen only looked at her in a helpless frightened sort of way, and kept repeating something in a whisper to herself that sounded like 'bread-and-butter, bread-and-butter,' and Alice felt that if there was to be any conversation at all, she must manage it herself. So she began rather timidly: 'Am I addressing the White Queen?'

'Well, yes, if you call that a-dressing,' The Queen said. 'It isn't MY notion of the thing, at all.'

Alice thought it would never do to have an argument at the very beginning of their conversation, so she smiled and said, 'If your Majesty will only tell me the right way to begin, I'll do it as well as I can.'

'But I don't want it done at all!' groaned the poor Queen. 'I've been a-dressing myself for the last two hours.'

It would have been all the better, as it seemed to Alice, if she had got some one else to dress her, she was so dreadfully untidy. 'Every single thing's crooked,' Alice thought to herself, 'and she's all over pins! — may I put your shawl straight for you?' she added aloud.

'I don't know what's the matter with it!' the Queen said, in a melancholy voice. 'It's out of temper, I think. I've pinned it here, and I've pinned it there, but there's no pleasing it!'

'It CAN'T go straight, you know, if you pin it all on one side,' Alice said, as she gently put it right for her; 'and, dear me, what a state your hair is in!'

'The brush has got entangled in it!' the Queen

said with a sigh. 'And I lost the comb yesterday.'

Alice carefully released the brush, and did her best to get the hair into order. 'Come, you look rather better now!' she said, after altering most of the pins. 'But really you should have a lady's maid!'

'I'm sure I'll take you with pleasure!' the Queen said. 'Twopence a week, and jam every other day.'

Alice couldn't help laughing, as she said, 'I don't want you to hire ME—and I don't care for jam.'

'It's very good jam,' said the Queen.

'Well, I don't want any TO-DAY, at any rate.'

'You couldn't have it if you DID want it,' the Queen said. 'The rule is, jam to-morrow and jam yesterday—but never jam to-day.'

'It MUST come sometimes to "jam to-day,"' Alice objected.

'No, it can't,' said the Queen. 'It's jam every OTHER day: to-day isn't any OTHER day, you know.'

'I don't understand you,' said Alice. 'It's dreadfully confusing!'

'That's the effect of living backwards,' the Queen said kindly: 'It always makes one a little giddy at first—'

'Living backwards!' Alice repeated in great astonishment. 'I never heard of such a thing!'

'—but there's one great advantage in it, that one's memory works both ways.'

'I'm sure MINE only works one way,' Alice remarked. 'I can't remember things before they happen.'

'It's a poor sort of memory that only works backwards,' the Queen remarked.

'What sort of things do YOU remember best?' Alice ventured to ask.

'Oh, things that happened the week after next,' the Queen replied in a careless tone. 'For instance, now,' she went on, sticking a large piece of plaster [band-aid] on her finger as she spoke, 'there's the King's Messenger. He's in prison now, being punished: and the trial doesn't even begin till next Wednesday: and of course the crime comes last of all.'

'Suppose he never commits the crime?' said

Alice.

'That would be all the better, wouldn't it?' the Queen said, as she bound the plaster round her finger with a bit of ribbon.

Alice felt there was no denying THAT. 'Of course it would be all the better,' she said: 'but it wouldn't be all the better his being punished.'

'You're wrong THERE, at any rate,' said the Queen: 'were YOU ever punished?'

'Only for faults,' said Alice.

'And you were all the better for it, I know!' the Queen said triumphantly.

'Yes, but then I HAD done the things I was punished for,' said Alice: 'that makes all the difference.'

'But if you HADN'T done them,' the Queen said, 'that would have been better still; better, and better, and better!' Her voice went higher with each 'better,' till it got quite to a squeak at last.

Alice was just beginning to say 'There's a mistake somewhere—,' when the Queen began screaming so loud that she had to leave the sentence unfinished. 'Oh, oh, oh!' shouted the

Queen, shaking her hand about as if she wanted to shake it off. 'My finger's bleeding! Oh, oh, oh, oh!'

Her screams were so exactly like the whistle of a steam-engine, that Alice had to hold both her hands over her ears.

'What IS the matter?' she said, as soon as there was a chance of making herself heard. 'Have you pricked your finger?'

'I haven't pricked it YET,' the Queen said, 'but I soon shall—oh, oh, oh!'

'When do you expect to do it?' Alice asked, feeling very much inclined to laugh.

'When I fasten my shawl again,' the poor Queen groaned out: 'the brooch will come undone directly. Oh, oh!' As she said the words the brooch flew open, and the Queen clutched wildly at it, and tried to clasp it again.

'Take care!' cried Alice. 'You're holding it all crooked!' And she caught at the brooch; but it was too late: the pin had slipped, and the Queen had pricked her finger.

'That accounts for the bleeding, you see,' she

said to Alice with a smile. 'Now you understand the way things happen here.'

'But why don't you scream now?' Alice asked, holding her hands ready to put over her ears again.

'Why, I've done all the screaming already,' said the Queen. 'What would be the good of having it all over again?'

By this time it was getting light. 'The crow must have flown away, I think,' said Alice: 'I'm so glad it's gone. I thought it was the night coming on.'

'I wish *I* could manage to be glad!' the Queen said. 'Only I never can remember the rule. You must be very happy, living in this wood, and being glad whenever you like!'

'Only it is so VERY lonely here!' Alice said in a melancholy voice; and at the thought of her loneliness two large tears came rolling down her cheeks.

'Oh, don't go on like that!' cried the poor Queen, wringing her hands in despair. 'Consider what a great girl you are. Consider what a long way you've come to-day. Consider what o'clock it is. Consider anything, only don't cry!'

Alice could not help laughing at this, even in the midst of her tears. 'Can YOU keep from crying by considering things?' she asked.

'That's the way it's done,' the Queen said with great decision: 'nobody can do two things at once, you know. Let's consider your age to begin with—how old are you?'

'I'm seven and a half exactly.'

'You needn't say "exactually,"' the Queen remarked: 'I can believe it without that. Now I'll give YOU something to believe. I'm just one hundred and one, five months and a day.'

'I can't believe THAT!' said Alice.

'Can't you?' the Queen said in a pitying tone. 'Try again: draw a long breath, and shut your eyes.'

Alice laughed. 'There's no use trying,' she said: 'one CAN'T believe impossible things.'

'I daresay you haven't had much practice,' said the Queen. 'When I was your age, I always did it for half-an-hour a day. Why, sometimes I've believed as many as six impossible things before breakfast. There goes the shawl again!'

The brooch had come undone as she spoke, and a sudden gust of wind blew the Queen's shawl across a little brook. The Queen spread out her arms again, and went flying after it, and this time she succeeded in catching it for herself. 'I've got it!' she cried in a triumphant tone. 'Now you shall see me pin it on again, all by myself!'

'Then I hope your finger is better now?' Alice said very politely, as she crossed the little brook after the Queen.

\*　　\*　　\*　　\*　　\*　　\*　　\*

　\*　　\*　　\*　　\*　　\*　　\*

\*　　\*　　\*　　\*　　\*　　\*　　\*

'Oh, much better!' cried the Queen, her voice rising to a squeak as she went on. 'Much be-etter! Be-etter! Be-e-e-etter! Be-e-ehh!' The last word ended in a long bleat, so like a sheep that Alice quite startled.

She looked at the Queen, who seemed to have suddenly wrapped herself up in wool. Alice rubbed her eyes, and looked again. She couldn't make out what had happened at all. Was she in a shop? And was that really—was it really a SHEEP that was sitting on the other side of the counter? Rub as she could, she could make nothing more of it: she was in a little dark shop, leaning with her elbows on the counter, and opposite to her was an old Sheep, sitting in an arm-chair knitting, and every now and then leaving off to look at her through a great pair of spectacles.

'What is it you want to buy?' the Sheep said at last, looking up for a moment from her knitting.

'I don't QUITE know yet,' Alice said, very gently. 'I should like to look all round me first, if I might.'

'You may look in front of you, and on both sides, if you like,' said the Sheep: 'but you can't look ALL round you—unless you've got eyes at the back of your head.'

But these, as it happened, Alice had NOT got: so she contented herself with turning round, looking at the shelves as she came to them.

The shop seemed to be full of all manner of curious things—but the oddest part of it all was, that whenever she looked hard at any shelf, to make out exactly what it had on it, that particular shelf was always quite empty: though the others round it were crowded as full as they could hold.

'Things flow about so here!' she said at last in a plaintive tone, after she had spent a minute or so in vainly pursuing a large bright thing, that looked sometimes like a doll and sometimes like a work-box, and was always in the shelf next above the one she was looking at. 'And this one is the most provoking of all—but I'll tell you what—' she added, as a sudden thought struck her, 'I'll follow it up to the very top shelf of all. It'll puzzle it to go through the ceiling, I expect!'

But even this plan failed: the 'thing' went through the ceiling as quietly as possible, as if it were quite used to it.

'Are you a child or a teetotum?' the Sheep said, as she took up another pair of needles. 'You'll make me giddy soon, if you go on turning round like that.' She was now working with fourteen pairs at once, and Alice couldn't help looking at her in great astonishment.

'How CAN she knit with so many?' the puzzled child thought to herself. 'She gets more and more like a porcupine every minute!'

'Can you row?' the Sheep asked, handing her a pair of knitting-needles as she spoke.

'Yes, a little—but not on land—and not with needles—' Alice was beginning to say, when suddenly the needles turned into oars in her hands, and she found they were in a little boat, gliding along between banks: so there was nothing for it but to do her best.

'Feather!' cried the Sheep, as she took up another pair of needles.

This didn't sound like a remark that needed any answer, so Alice said nothing, but pulled away. There was something very queer about the water, she thought, as every now and then the oars got fast in it, and would hardly come out again.

'Feather! Feather!' the Sheep cried again, taking more needles. 'You'll be catching a crab directly.'

'A dear little crab!' thought Alice. 'I should like

that.'

'Didn't you hear me say "Feather"?' the Sheep cried angrily, taking up quite a bunch of needles.

'Indeed I did,' said Alice: 'you've said it very often—and very loud. Please, where ARE the crabs?'

'In the water, of course!' said the Sheep, sticking some of the needles into her hair, as her hands were full. 'Feather, I say!'

'WHY do you say "feather" so often?' Alice asked at last, rather vexed. 'I'm not a bird!'

'You are,' said the Sheep: 'you're a little goose.'

This offended Alice a little, so there was no more conversation for a minute or two, while the boat glided gently on, sometimes among beds of weeds (which made the oars stick fast in the water, worse then ever), and sometimes under trees, but always with the same tall river-banks frowning over their heads.

'Oh, please! There are some scented rushes!' Alice cried in a sudden transport of delight. 'There really are—and SUCH beauties!'

'You needn't say "please" to ME about 'em,' the Sheep said, without looking up from her knitting:

'I didn't put 'em there, and I'm not going to take 'em away.'

'No, but I meant—please, may we wait and pick some?' Alice pleaded. 'If you don't mind stopping the boat for a minute.'

'How am *I* to stop it?' said the Sheep. 'If you leave off rowing, it'll stop of itself.'

So the boat was left to drift down the stream as it would, till it glided gently in among the waving rushes. And then the little sleeves were carefully rolled up, and the little arms were plunged in elbow-deep to get the rushes a good long way down before breaking them off—and for a while Alice forgot all about the Sheep and the knitting, as she bent over the side of the boat, with just the ends of her tangled hair dipping into the water—while with bright eager eyes she caught at one bunch after another of the darling scented rushes.

'I only hope the boat won't tipple over!' she said to herself. 'Oh, WHAT a lovely one! Only I couldn't quite reach it.' 'And it certainly DID seem a little provoking ('almost as if it happened on purpose,' she thought) that, though she managed to pick plenty of beautiful rushes as the boat glided by, there was always a more lovely one that she couldn't reach.

'The prettiest are always further!' she said at last, with a sigh at the obstinacy of the rushes in growing so far off, as, with flushed cheeks and dripping hair and hands, she scrambled back into her place, and began to arrange her new-found treasures.

What mattered it to her just then that the rushes had begun to fade, and to lose all their scent and beauty, from the very moment that she picked them? Even real scented rushes, you know, last only a very little while—and these, being dream-rushes, melted away almost like snow, as they lay in heaps at her feet—but Alice hardly noticed this, there were so many other curious things to think about.

They hadn't gone much farther before the blade of one of the oars got fast in the water and WOULDN'T come out again (so Alice explained it afterwards), and the consequence was that the handle of it caught her under the chin, and, in spite of a series of little shrieks of 'Oh, oh, oh!' from poor Alice, it swept her straight off the seat, and down among the heap of rushes.

However, she wasn't hurt, and was soon up again: the Sheep went on with her knitting all the while, just as if nothing had happened. 'That was a nice crab you caught!' she remarked, as Alice got back into her place, very much relieved to find herself still in the boat.

'Was it? I didn't see it,' Said Alice, peeping cautiously over the side of the boat into the dark water. 'I wish it hadn't let go—I should so like to see a little crab to take home with me!' But the Sheep only laughed scornfully, and went on with her knitting.

'Are there many crabs here?' said Alice.

'Crabs, and all sorts of things,' said the Sheep: 'plenty of choice, only make up your mind. Now, what DO you want to buy?'

'To buy!' Alice echoed in a tone that was half astonished and half frightened—for the oars, and the boat, and the river, had vanished all in a moment, and she was back again in the little dark shop.

'I should like to buy an egg, please,' she said timidly. 'How do you sell them?'

'Fivepence farthing for one—Twopence for two,' the Sheep replied.

'Then two are cheaper than one?' Alice said in a surprised tone, taking out her purse.

'Only you MUST eat them both, if you buy two,' said the Sheep.

'Then I'll have ONE, please,' said Alice, as she put the money down on the counter. For she thought to herself, 'They mightn't be at all nice, you know.'

The Sheep took the money, and put it away in a box: then she said 'I never put things into people's hands—that would never do—you must get it for yourself.' And so saying, she went off to the other end of the shop, and set the egg upright on a shelf.

'I wonder WHY it wouldn't do?' thought Alice, as she groped her way among the tables and chairs, for the shop was very dark towards the end. 'The egg seems to get further away the more

I walk towards it. Let me see, is this a chair? Why, it's got branches, I declare! How very odd to find trees growing here! And actually here's a little brook! Well, this is the very queerest shop I ever saw!'

\* \* \* \* \* \* \*
\* \* \* \* \* \*
\* \* \* \* \* \* \*

So she went on, wondering more and more at every step, as everything turned into a tree the moment she came up to it, and she quite expected the egg to do the same.

# CHAPTER VI
# Humpty Dumpty

However, the egg only got larger and larger, and more and more human: when she had come within a few yards of it, she saw that it had eyes and a nose and mouth; and when she had come close to it, she saw clearly that it was HUMPTY DUMPTY himself. 'It can't be anybody else!' she said to herself. 'I'm as certain of it, as if his name were written all over his face.'

It might have been written a hundred times, easily, on that enormous face. Humpty Dumpty was sitting with his legs crossed, like a Turk, on the top of a high wall—such a narrow one that Alice quite wondered how he could keep his balance—and, as his eyes were steadily fixed in the opposite direction, and he didn't take the least notice of her, she thought he must be a stuffed figure after all.

'And how exactly like an egg he is!' she said aloud, standing with her hands ready to catch him, for she was every moment expecting him to fall.

'It's VERY provoking,' Humpty Dumpty said after a long silence, looking away from Alice as he spoke, 'to be called an egg—VERY!'

'I said you LOOKED like an egg, Sir,' Alice gently explained. 'And some eggs are very pretty, you know' she added, hoping to turn her remark into a sort of a compliment.

'Some people,' said Humpty Dumpty, looking away from her as usual, 'have no more sense than a baby!'

Alice didn't know what to say to this: it wasn't at all like conversation, she thought, as he never said anything to HER; in fact, his last remark was evidently addressed to a tree—so she stood and softly repeated to herself:—

'Humpty Dumpty sat on a wall:
Humpty Dumpty had a great fall.
All the King's horses and all the King's men
Couldn't put Humpty Dumpty in his place again.'

'That last line is much too long for the poetry,' she added, almost out loud, forgetting that Humpty Dumpty would hear her.

'Don't stand there chattering to yourself like that,' Humpty Dumpty said, looking at her for the first time, 'but tell me your name and your business.'

'My NAME is Alice, but—'

'It's a stupid enough name!' Humpty Dumpty interrupted impatiently. 'What does it mean?'

'MUST a name mean something?' Alice asked doubtfully.

'Of course it must,' Humpty Dumpty said with a short laugh: 'MY name means the shape I am—and a good handsome shape it is, too. With a name like yours, you might be any shape, almost.'

'Why do you sit out here all alone?' said Alice, not wishing to begin an argument.

'Why, because there's nobody with me!' cried Humpty Dumpty. 'Did you think I didn't know the answer to THAT? Ask another.'

'Don't you think you'd be safer down on the ground?' Alice went on, not with any idea of making another riddle, but simply in her good-natured anxiety for the queer creature. 'That wall is so VERY narrow!'

'What tremendously easy riddles you ask!' Humpty Dumpty growled out. 'Of course I don't think so! Why, if ever I DID fall off—which there's no chance of—but IF I did—' Here he pursed up his lips and looked so solemn and grand that Alice could hardly help laughing. 'IF I did fall,' he went on, 'THE KING HAS PROMISED ME—ah, you may turn pale, if you like! You didn't think I was going to say that, did you? THE KING HAS PROMISED ME— WITH HIS VERY OWN MOUTH—to—to—'

'To send all his horses and all his men,' Alice interrupted, rather unwisely.

'Now I declare that's too bad!' Humpty Dumpty cried, breaking into a sudden passion. 'You've been listening at doors—and behind trees—and down chimneys—or you couldn't have known it!'

'I haven't, indeed!' Alice said very gently. 'It's in a book.'

'Ah, well! They may write such things in a

BOOK,' Humpty Dumpty said in a calmer tone. 'That's what you call a History of England, that is. Now, take a good look at me! I'm one that has spoken to a King, *I* am: mayhap you'll never see such another: and to show you I'm not proud, you may shake hands with me!' And he grinned almost from ear to ear, as he leant forwards (and as nearly as possible fell off the wall in doing so) and offered Alice his hand. She watched him a little anxiously as she took it. 'If he smiled much more, the ends of his mouth might meet behind,' she thought: 'and then I don't know what would happen to his head! I'm afraid it would come off!'

'Yes, all his horses and all his men,' Humpty Dumpty went on. 'They'd pick me up again in a minute, THEY would! However, this conversation is going on a little too fast: let's go back to the last remark but one.'

'I'm afraid I can't quite remember it,' Alice said very politely.

'In that case we start fresh,' said Humpty Dumpty, 'and it's my turn to choose a subject—' ('He talks about it just as if it was a game!' thought

Alice.) 'So here's a question for you. How old did you say you were?'

Alice made a short calculation, and said 'Seven years and six months.'

'Wrong!' Humpty Dumpty exclaimed triumphantly. 'You never said a word like it!'

'I though you meant "How old ARE you?"' Alice explained.

'If I'd meant that, I'd have said it,' said Humpty Dumpty.

Alice didn't want to begin another argument, so she said nothing.

'Seven years and six months!' Humpty Dumpty repeated thoughtfully. 'An uncomfortable sort of age. Now if you'd asked MY advice, I'd have said "Leave off at seven"—but it's too late now.'

'I never ask advice about growing,' Alice said indignantly.

'Too proud?' the other inquired.

Alice felt even more indignant at this suggestion. 'I mean,' she said, 'that one can't help growing older.'

'ONE can't, perhaps,' said Humpty Dumpty,

'but TWO can. With proper assistance, you might have left off at seven.'

'What a beautiful belt you've got on!' Alice suddenly remarked.

(They had had quite enough of the subject of age, she thought: and if they really were to take turns in choosing subjects, it was her turn now.) 'At least,' she corrected herself on second thoughts, 'a beautiful cravat, I should have said—no, a belt, I mean—I beg your pardon!' she added in dismay, for Humpty Dumpty looked thoroughly offended, and she began to wish she hadn't chosen that subject. 'If I only knew,' she thought to herself, 'which was neck and which was waist!'

Evidently Humpty Dumpty was very angry, though he said nothing for a minute or two. When he DID speak again, it was in a deep growl.

'It is a—MOST—PROVOKING—thing,' he said at last, 'when a person doesn't know a cravat from a belt!'

'I know it's very ignorant of me,' Alice said, in so humble a tone that Humpty Dumpty relented.

'It's a cravat, child, and a beautiful one, as

you say. It's a present from the White King and Queen. There now!'

'Is it really?' said Alice, quite pleased to find that she HAD chosen a good subject, after all.

'They gave it me,' Humpty Dumpty continued thoughtfully, as he crossed one knee over the other and clasped his hands round it, 'they gave it me—for an un-birthday present.'

'I beg your pardon?' Alice said with a puzzled air.

'I'm not offended,' said Humpty Dumpty.
'I mean, what IS an un-birthday present?'

'A present given when it isn't your birthday, of course.'

Alice considered a little. 'I like birthday presents best,' she said at last.

'You don't know what you're talking about!' cried Humpty Dumpty. 'How many days are there in a year?'

'Three hundred and sixty-five,' said Alice.

'And how many birthdays have you?'

'One.'

'And if you take one from three hundred and

sixty-five, what remains?'

'Three hundred and sixty-four, of course.'

Humpty Dumpty looked doubtful. 'I'd rather see that done on paper,' he said.

Alice couldn't help smiling as she took out her memorandum-book, and worked the sum for him:

$$\begin{array}{r}365\\1\\\hline 364\\\hline\end{array}$$

Humpty Dumpty took the book, and looked at it carefully. 'That seems to be done right—' he began.

'You're holding it upside down!' Alice interrupted.

'To be sure I was!' Humpty Dumpty said gaily, as she turned it round for him. 'I thought it looked a little queer. As I was saying, that SEEMS to be done right—though I haven't time to look it over thoroughly just now—and that shows that there are three hundred and sixty-four days when you might get un-birthday presents—'

'Certainly,' said Alice.

'And only ONE for birthday presents, you know. There's glory for you!'

'I don't know what you mean by "glory,"' Alice said.

Humpty Dumpty smiled contemptuously. 'Of course you don't—till I tell you. I meant "there's a nice knock-down argument for you!"'

'But "glory" doesn't mean "a nice knock-down argument,"' Alice objected.

'When *I* use a word,' Humpty Dumpty said in rather a scornful tone, 'It means just what I choose it to mean—neither more nor less.'

'The question is,' said Alice, 'whether you CAN make words mean so many different things.'

'The question is,' said Humpty Dumpty, 'which is to be master—that's all.'

Alice was too much puzzled to say anything, so after a minute Humpty Dumpty began again. 'They've a temper, some of them—particularly verbs, they're the proudest—adjectives you can do anything with, but not verbs—however, *I* can manage the whole lot of them! Impenetrability! That's what *I* say!'

'Would you tell me, please,' said Alice 'what that means?'

'Now you talk like a reasonable child,' said Humpty Dumpty, looking very much pleased. 'I meant by "impenetrability" that we've had enough of that subject, and it would be just as well if you'd mention what you mean to do next, as I suppose you don't mean to stop here all the rest of your life.'

'That's a great deal to make one word mean,' Alice said in a thoughtful tone.

'When I make a word do a lot of work like that,' said Humpty Dumpty, 'I always pay it extra.'

'Oh!' said Alice. She was too much puzzled to make any other remark.

'Ah, you should see 'em come round me of a Saturday night,' Humpty Dumpty went on, wagging his head gravely from side to side: 'for to get their wages, you know.'

(Alice didn't venture to ask what he paid them with; and so you see I can't tell YOU.)

'You seem very clever at explaining words, Sir,' said Alice. 'Would you kindly tell me the meaning of the poem called "Jabberwocky"?'

'Let's hear it,' said Humpty Dumpty. 'I can explain all the poems that were ever invented—and a good many that haven't been invented just yet.'

This sounded very hopeful, so Alice repeated the first verse:

'Twas brillig, and the slithy toves
Did gyre and gimble in the wabe;
All mimsy were the borogoves,
And the mome raths outgrabe.

'That's enough to begin with,' Humpty Dumpty interrupted: 'there are plenty of hard words there. "BRILLIG" means four o'clock in the afternoon- the time when you begin BROILING things for dinner.'

'That'll do very well,' said Alice: 'and "SLITHY"?'

'Well, "SLITHY" means "lithe and slimy." "Lithe" is the same as "active." You see it's like a portmanteau—there are two meanings packed up into one word.'

'I see it now,' Alice remarked thoughtfully: 'and what are "TOVES"?'

'Well, "TOVES" are something like badgers-they're something like lizards—and they're something like corkscrews.'

'They must be very curious looking creatures.'

'They are that,' said Humpty Dumpty: 'also they make their nests under sun-dials—also they live on cheese.'

'And what's the "GYRE" and to "GIMBLE"?'

'To "GYRE" is to go round and round like a gyroscope. To "GIMBLE" is to make holes like a gimlet.'

'And "THE WABE" is the grass-plot round a sun-dial, I suppose?' said Alice, surprised at her own ingenuity.

'Of course it is. It's called "WABE," you know, because it goes a long way before it, and a long way behind it—'

'And a long way beyond it on each side,' Alice added. 'Exactly so. Well, then, "MIMSY" is "flimsy and miserable" (there's another portmanteau for you). And a "BOROGOVE" is a thin shabby-looking bird with its feathers sticking out all round—something like a live mop.'

'And then "MOME RATHS"?' said Alice. 'I'm afraid I'm giving you a great deal of trouble.'

'Well, a "RATH" is a sort of green pig: but "MOME" I'm not certain about. I think it's short for "from home"—meaning that they'd lost their way, you know.'

'And what does "OUTGRABE" mean?'

'Well, "OUTGRABING" is something between bellowing and whistling, with a kind of sneeze in the middle: however, you'll hear it done, maybe—down in the wood yonder—and when you've once heard it you'll be QUITE content. Who's been repeating all that hard stuff to you?'

'I read it in a book,' said Alice. 'But I had some poetry repeated to me, much easier than that, by—Tweedledee, I think it was.'

'As to poetry, you know,' said Humpty Dumpty, stretching out one of his great hands, 'I can repeat poetry as well as other folk, if it comes to that—'

'Oh, it needn't come to that!' Alice hastily said, hoping to keep him from beginning.

'The piece I'm going to repeat,' he went on without noticing her remark, 'was written entirely for your amusement.'

Alice felt that in that case she really OUGHT to listen to it, so she sat down, and said 'Thank you' rather sadly.

'In winter, when the fields are white,

I sing this song for your delight—

only I don't sing it,' he added, as an explanation.

'I see you don't,' said Alice.

'If you can SEE whether I'm singing or not, you've sharper eyes than most.' Humpty Dumpty remarked severely. Alice was silent.

'In spring, when woods are getting green,

I'll try and tell you what I mean.'

'Thank you very much,' said Alice.

'In summer, when the days are long,
Perhaps you'll understand the song:
In autumn, when the leaves are brown,
Take pen and ink, and write it down.'

'I will, if I can remember it so long,' said Alice.
'You needn't go on making remarks like that,' Humpty Dumpty said: 'they're not sensible, and they put me out.'

'I sent a message to the fish:
I told them "This is what I wish."

The little fishes of the sea,

They sent an answer back to me.

The little fishes' answer was

"We cannot do it, Sir, because—"'

'I'm afraid I don't quite understand,' said Alice.
'It gets easier further on,' Humpty Dumpty re-

plied.

'I sent to them again to say
"It will be better to obey."

The fishes answered with a grin,
"Why, what a temper you are in!"

I told them once, I told them twice:
They would not listen to advice.
I took a kettle large and new,
Fit for the deed I had to do.

My heart went hop, my heart went thump;
I filled the kettle at the pump.

Then some one came to me and said,
"The little fishes are in bed."

I said to him, I said it plain,
"Then you must wake them up again."

I said it very loud and clear;

I went and shouted in his ear.'

Humpty Dumpty raised his voice almost to a scream as he repeated this verse, and Alice thought with a shudder, 'I wouldn't have been the messenger for ANYTHING!'

'But he was very stiff and proud;
He said "You needn't shout so loud!"

And he was very proud and stiff;
He said "I'd go and wake them, if—"

I took a corkscrew from the shelf:
I went to wake them up myself.

And when I found the door was locked,
I pulled and pushed and kicked and knocked.

And when I found the door was shut,
I tried to turn the handle, but—'

There was a long pause.

'Is that all?' Alice timidly asked.

'That's all,' said Humpty Dumpty. 'Good-bye.'

This was rather sudden, Alice thought: but, after such a VERY strong hint that she ought to be going, she felt that it would hardly be civil to stay. So she got up, and held out her hand. 'Good-bye, till we meet again!' she said as cheerfully as she could.

'I shouldn't know you again if we DID meet,' Humpty Dumpty replied in a discontented tone, giving her one of his fingers to shake; 'you're so exactly like other people.'

'The face is what one goes by, generally,' Alice remarked in a thoughtful tone.

'That's just what I complain of,' said Humpty Dumpty. 'Your face is the same as everybody has—the two eyes, so—' (marking their places in the air with this thumb) 'nose in the middle, mouth under. It's always the same. Now if you had the two eyes on the same side of the nose, for instance—or the mouth at the top—that would be SOME help.'

'It wouldn't look nice,' Alice objected. But

Humpty Dumpty only shut his eyes and said 'Wait till you've tried.'

　　Alice waited a minute to see if he would speak again, but as he never opened his eyes or took any further notice of her, she said 'Good-bye!' once more, and, getting no answer to this, she quietly walked away: but she couldn't help saying to herself as she went, 'Of all the unsatisfactory—' (she repeated this aloud, as it was a great comfort to have such a long word to say) 'of all the unsatisfactory people I EVER met—' She never finished the sentence, for at this moment a heavy crash shook the forest from end to end.

# CHAPTER VII
# The Lion and the Unicorn

The next moment soldiers came running through the wood, at first in twos and threes, then ten or twenty together, and at last in such crowds that they seemed to fill the whole forest. Alice got behind a tree, for fear of being run over, and watched them go by.

She thought that in all her life she had never seen soldiers so uncertain on their feet: they were always tripping over something or other, and whenever one went down, several more always fell over him, so that the ground was soon covered with little heaps of men.

Then came the horses. Having four feet, these managed rather better than the foot-soldiers: but even THEY stumbled now and then; and it seemed to be a regular rule that, whenever a horse stumbled the rider fell off instantly. The confusion got worse every moment, and Alice was very glad to get out of the wood into an open place, where she found the White King seated on the ground, busily writing in his memorandum-book.

'I've sent them all!' the King cried in a tone of delight, on seeing Alice. 'Did you happen to meet any soldiers, my dear, as you came through the wood?'

'Yes, I did,' said Alice: 'several thousand, I should think.'

'Four thousand two hundred and seven, that's the exact number,' the King said, referring to his book. 'I couldn't send all the horses, you know, because two of them are wanted in the game. And I haven't sent the two Messengers, either. They're both gone to the town. Just look along the road, and tell me if you can see either of them.'

'I see nobody on the road,' said Alice.

'I only wish *I* had such eyes,' the King remarked in a fretful tone. 'To be able to see Nobody! And at that distance, too! Why, it's as much as *I* can do to see real people, by this light!'

All this was lost on Alice, who was still looking intently along the road, shading her eyes with one hand. 'I see somebody now!' she exclaimed at last.

'But he's coming very slowly—and what curious attitudes he goes into!' (For the messenger kept skipping up and down, and wriggling like an eel, as he came along, with his great hands spread out like fans on each side.)

'Not at all,' said the King. 'He's an Anglo-Saxon Messenger—and those are Anglo-Saxon attitudes. He only does them when he's happy. His name is Haigha.' (He pronounced it so as to rhyme with 'mayor.')

'I love my love with an H,' Alice couldn't help beginning, 'because he is Happy. I hate him with an H, because he is Hideous. I fed him with—with—with Ham-sandwiches and Hay. His name is Haigha, and he lives—'

'He lives on the Hill,' the King remarked simply, without the least idea that he was joining in the game, while Alice was still hesitating for the name of a town beginning with H. 'The other Messenger's called Hatta. I must have TWO, you know—to come and go. One to come, and one to go.'

'I beg your pardon?' said Alice.

'It isn't respectable to beg,' said the King.

'I only meant that I didn't understand,' said Alice. 'Why one to come and one to go?'

'Didn't I tell you?' the King repeated impatiently. 'I must have Two—to fetch and carry. One to fetch, and one to carry.'

At this moment the Messenger arrived: he was far too much out of breath to say a word, and could only wave his hands about, and make the most fearful faces at the poor King.

'This young lady loves you with an H,' the King said, introducing Alice in the hope of turning off the Messenger's attention from himself—but it was no use—the Anglo-Saxon attitudes only got more extraordinary every moment, while the great eyes rolled wildly from side to side.

'You alarm me!' said the King. 'I feel faint— Give me a ham sandwich!'

On which the Messenger, to Alice's great amusement, opened a bag that hung round his neck, and handed a sandwich to the King, who devoured it greedily.

'Another sandwich!' said the King.

'There's nothing but hay left now,' the Messenger said, peeping into the bag.

'Hay, then,' the King murmured in a faint whisper.

Alice was glad to see that it revived him a good deal. 'There's nothing like eating hay when you're faint,' he remarked to her, as he munched away.

'I should think throwing cold water over you would be better,' Alice suggested: 'or some sal-volatile.'

'I didn't say there was nothing BETTER,' the King replied. 'I said there was nothing LIKE it.' Which Alice did not venture to deny.

'Who did you pass on the road?' the King went on, holding out his hand to the Messenger for some more hay.

'Nobody,' said the Messenger.

'Quite right,' said the King: 'this young lady saw him too. So of course Nobody walks slower than you.'

'I do my best,' the Messenger said in a sulky tone. 'I'm sure nobody walks much faster than I do!'

'He can't do that,' said the King, 'or else he'd have been here first. However, now you've got your breath, you may tell us what's happened in the town.'

'I'll whisper it,' said the Messenger, putting his hands to his mouth in the shape of a trumpet, and stooping so as to get close to the King's ear. Alice was sorry for this, as she wanted to hear the news too. However, instead of whispering, he simply shouted at the top of his voice 'They're at it again!'

'Do you call THAT a whisper?' cried the poor King, jumping up and shaking himself. 'If you do such a thing again, I'll have you buttered! It went through and through my head like an earthquake!'

'It would have to be a very tiny earthquake!' thought Alice. 'Who are at it again?' she ventured to ask.

'Why the Lion and the Unicorn, of course,' said the King.

'Fighting for the crown?'

'Yes, to be sure,' said the King: 'and the best of the joke is, that it's MY crown all the while! Let's run and see them.' And they trotted off, Alice repeating to herself, as she ran, the words of the old song:—

'The Lion and the Unicorn were fighting for the crown:
The Lion beat the Unicorn all round the town.
Some gave them white bread, some gave them brown;
Some gave them plum-cake and drummed them out of town.'

'Does—the one—that wins—get the crown?' she asked, as well as she could, for the run was putting her quite out of breath.

'Dear me, no!' said the King. 'What an idea!'
'Would you—be good enough,' Alice panted out, after running a little further, 'to stop a minute—just to get—one's breath again?'
'I'm GOOD enough,' the King said, 'only I'm not strong enough. You see, a minute goes by so fearfully quick. You might as well try to stop a

Bandersnatch!'

Alice had no more breath for talking, so they trotted on in silence, till they came in sight of a great crowd, in the middle of which the Lion and Unicorn were fighting. They were in such a cloud of dust, that at first Alice could not make out which was which: but she soon managed to distinguish the Unicorn by his horn.

They placed themselves close to where Hatta, the other messenger, was standing watching the fight, with a cup of tea in one hand and a piece of bread-and-butter in the other.

'He's only just out of prison, and he hadn't finished his tea when he was sent in,' Haigha whispered to Alice: 'and they only give them oyster-shells in there—so you see he's very hungry and thirsty. How are you, dear child?' he went on, putting his arm affectionately round Hatta's neck.

Hatta looked round and nodded, and went on with his bread and butter.

'Were you happy in prison, dear child?' said Haigha.

Hatta looked round once more, and this time

a tear or two trickled down his cheek: but not a word would he say.

'Speak, can't you!' Haigha cried impatiently. But Hatta only munched away, and drank some more tea.

'Speak, won't you!' cried the King. 'How are they getting on with the fight?'

Hatta made a desperate effort, and swallowed a large piece of bread-and-butter. 'They're getting on very well,' he said in a choking voice: 'each of them has been down about eighty-seven times.'

'Then I suppose they'll soon bring the white bread and the brown?' Alice ventured to remark.

'It's waiting for 'em now,' said Hatta: 'this is a bit of it as I'm eating.'

There was a pause in the fight just then, and the Lion and the Unicorn sat down, panting, while the King called out 'Ten minutes allowed for refreshments!' Haigha and Hatta set to work at once, carrying rough trays of white and brown bread. Alice took a piece to taste, but it was VERY dry.

'I don't think they'll fight any more to-day,' the

King said to Hatta: 'go and order the drums to begin.' And Hatta went bounding away like a grasshopper.

For a minute or two Alice stood silent, watching him. Suddenly she brightened up. 'Look, look!' she cried, pointing eagerly. 'There's the White Queen running across the country! She came flying out of the wood over yonder—How fast those Queens CAN run!'

'There's some enemy after her, no doubt,' the King said, without even looking round. 'That wood's full of them.'

'But aren't you going to run and help her?' Alice asked, very much surprised at his taking it so quietly.

'No use, no use!' said the King. 'She runs so fearfully quick. You might as well try to catch a Bandersnatch! But I'll make a memorandum about her, if you like—She's a dear good creature,' he repeated softly to himself, as he opened his memorandum-book. 'Do you spell "creature" with a double "e"?'

At this moment the Unicorn sauntered by

them, with his hands in his pockets. 'I had the best of it this time?' he said to the King, just glancing at him as he passed.

'A little—a little,' the King replied, rather nervously. 'You shouldn't have run him through with your horn, you know.'

'It didn't hurt him,' the Unicorn said carelessly, and he was going on, when his eye happened to fall upon Alice: he turned round rather instantly, and stood for some time looking at her with an air of the deepest disgust.

'What—is—this?' he said at last.

'This is a child!' Haigha replied eagerly, coming in front of Alice to introduce her, and spreading out both his hands towards her in an Anglo-Saxon attitude. 'We only found it to-day. It's as large as life, and twice as natural!'

'I always thought they were fabulous monsters!' said the Unicorn. 'Is it alive?'

'It can talk,' said Haigha, solemnly.

The Unicorn looked dreamily at Alice, and said 'Talk, child.'

Alice could not help her lips curling up into

a smile as she began: 'Do you know, I always thought Unicorns were fabulous monsters, too! I never saw one alive before!'

'Well, now that we HAVE seen each other,' said the Unicorn, 'If you'll believe in me, I'll believe in you. Is that a bargain?'

'Yes, if you like,' said Alice.

'Come, fetch out the plum-cake, old man!' the Unicorn went on, turning from her to the King. 'None of your brown bread for me!'

'Certainly—certainly!' the King muttered, and beckoned to Haigha. 'Open the bag!' he whispered. 'Quick! Not that one—that's full of hay!' Haigha took a large cake out of the bag, and gave it to Alice to hold, while he got out a dish and carving-knife. How they all came out of it Alice couldn't guess. It was just like a conjuring-trick, she thought.

The Lion had joined them while this was going on: he looked very tired and sleepy, and his eyes were half shut. 'What's this!' he said, blinking lazily at Alice, and speaking in a deep hollow tone that sounded like the tolling of a great bell.

'Ah, what IS it, now?' the Unicorn cried eagerly. 'You'll never guess! *I* couldn't.'

The Lion looked at Alice wearily. 'Are you animal—vegetable—or mineral?' he said, yawning at every other word.

'It's a fabulous monster!' the Unicorn cried out, before Alice could reply.

'Then hand round the plum-cake, Monster,' the Lion said, lying down and putting his chin on this paws. 'And sit down, both of you,' (to the King and the Unicorn): 'fair play with the cake, you know!'

The King was evidently very uncomfortable at having to sit down between the two great creatures; but there was no other place for him.

'What a fight we might have for the crown, NOW!' the Unicorn said, looking slyly up at the crown, which the poor King was nearly shaking off his head, he trembled so much.

'I should win easy,' said the Lion.

'I'm not so sure of that,' said the Unicorn.

'Why, I beat you all round the town, you chicken!' the Lion replied angrily, half getting up as he spoke.

Here the King interrupted, to prevent the quarrel going on: he was very nervous, and his voice quite quivered. 'All round the town?' he said. 'That's a good long way. Did you go by the old bridge, or the market-place? You get the best view by the old bridge.'

'I'm sure I don't know,' the Lion growled out as he lay down again. 'There was too much dust to see anything. What a time the Monster is, cutting up that cake!'

Alice had seated herself on the bank of a little brook, with the great dish on her knees, and was sawing away diligently with the knife. 'It's very provoking!' she said, in reply to the Lion (she was getting quite used to being called 'the Monster'). 'I've cut several slices already, but they always join on again!'

'You don't know how to manage Looking-glass cakes,' the Unicorn remarked. 'Hand it round first, and cut it afterwards.'

This sounded nonsense, but Alice very obediently got up, and carried the dish round, and the cake divided itself into three pieces as she did so. 'NOW cut it up,' said the Lion, as she returned to her place with the empty dish.

'I say, this isn't fair!' cried the Unicorn, as Alice sat with the knife in her hand, very much puzzled how to begin. 'The Monster has given the Lion twice as much as me!'

'She's kept none for herself, anyhow,' said the Lion. 'Do you like plum-cake, Monster?'

But before Alice could answer him, the drums began.

Where the noise came from, she couldn't make out: the air seemed full of it, and it rang through and through her head till she felt quite deafened. She started to her feet and sprang across the little brook in her terror,

\*   \*   \*   \*   \*   \*   \*
   \*   \*   \*   \*   \*   \*
\*   \*   \*   \*   \*   \*   \*

and had just time to see the Lion and the Unicorn rise to their feet, with angry looks at being interrupted in their feast, before she dropped to her knees, and put her hands over her ears, vainly

trying to shut out the dreadful uproar.
'If THAT doesn't "drum them out of town,"' she thought to herself, 'nothing ever will!'

# CHAPTER VIII
## 'It's my own Invention'

After a while the noise seemed gradually to die away, till all was dead silence, and Alice lifted up her head in some alarm. There was no one to be seen, and her first thought was that she must have been dreaming about the Lion and the Unicorn and those queer Anglo-Saxon Messengers. However, there was the great dish still lying at her feet, on which she had tried to cut the plum-cake, 'So I wasn't dreaming, after all,' she said to herself, 'unless—unless we're all part of the same dream. Only I do hope it's MY dream, and not the Red King's! I don't like belonging to another person's dream,' she went on in a rather complaining tone: 'I've a great mind to go and wake him, and see what happens!'

At this moment her thoughts were interrupted by a loud shouting of 'Ahoy! Ahoy! Check!' and a Knight dressed in crimson armour came galloping down upon her, brandishing a great club. Just as he reached her, the horse stopped suddenly: 'You're my prisoner!' the Knight cried, as he tumbled off his horse.

Startled as she was, Alice was more frightened for him than for herself at the moment, and watched him with some anxiety as he mounted again. As soon as he was comfortably in the saddle, he began once more 'You're my—' but here another voice broke in 'Ahoy! Ahoy! Check!' and Alice looked round in some surprise for the new enemy.

This time it was a White Knight. He drew up at Alice's side, and tumbled off his horse just as the Red Knight had done: then he got on again, and the two Knights sat and looked at each other for some time without speaking. Alice looked from one to the other in some bewilderment.

'She's MY prisoner, you know!' the Red Knight said at last.

'Yes, but then *I* came and rescued her!' the White Knight replied.

'Well, we must fight for her, then,' said the Red Knight, as he took up his helmet (which hung from the saddle, and was something the shape of a horse's head), and put it on.

'You will observe the Rules of Battle, of course?' the White Knight remarked, putting on his helmet too.

'I always do,' said the Red Knight, and they began banging away at each other with such fury that Alice got behind a tree to be out of the way of the blows.

'I wonder, now, what the Rules of Battle are,' she said to herself, as she watched the fight, timidly peeping out from her hiding-place: 'one Rule seems to be, that if one Knight hits the other, he knocks him off his horse, and if he misses, he tumbles off himself—and another Rule seems to be that they hold their clubs with their arms, as if they were Punch and Judy—What a noise they make when they tumble! Just like a whole set of fire-irons falling into the fender! And how quiet the horses are! They let them get on and off them just as if they were tables!'

Another Rule of Battle, that Alice had not noticed, seemed to be that they always fell on their heads, and the battle ended with their both falling off in this way, side by side: when they got up again, they shook hands, and then the Red Knight mounted and galloped off.

'It was a glorious victory, wasn't it?' said the White Knight, as he came up panting.

'I don't know,' Alice said doubtfully. 'I don't want to be anybody's prisoner. I want to be a Queen.'

'So you will, when you've crossed the next brook,' said the White Knight. 'I'll see you safe to the end of the wood—and then I must go back, you know. That's the end of my move.'

'Thank you very much,' said Alice. 'May I help you off with your helmet?' It was evidently more than he could manage by himself; however, she managed to shake him out of it at last.

'Now one can breathe more easily,' said the Knight, putting back his shaggy hair with both hands, and turning his gentle face and large mild eyes to Alice. She thought she had never seen such a strange-looking soldier in all her life.

He was dressed in tin armour, which seemed

to fit him very badly, and he had a queer-shaped little deal box fastened across his shoulder, upside-down, and with the lid hanging open. Alice looked at it with great curiosity.

'I see you're admiring my little box.' the Knight said in a friendly tone. 'It's my own invention—to keep clothes and sandwiches in. You see I carry it upside-down, so that the rain can't get in.'

'But the things can get OUT,' Alice gently remarked. 'Do you know the lid's open?'

'I didn't know it,' the Knight said, a shade of vexation passing over his face. 'Then all the things must have fallen out! And the box is no use without them.' He unfastened it as he spoke, and was just going to throw it into the bushes, when a sudden thought seemed to strike him, and he hung it carefully on a tree. 'Can you guess why I did that?' he said to Alice.

Alice shook her head.

'In hopes some bees may make a nest in it—then I should get the honey.'

'But you've got a bee-hive—or something like one—fastened to the saddle,' said Alice.

'Yes, it's a very good bee-hive,' the Knight said in a discontented tone, 'one of the best kind. But not a single bee has come near it yet. And the other thing is a mouse-trap. I suppose the mice keep the bees out—or the bees keep the mice out, I don't know which.'

'I was wondering what the mouse-trap was for,' said Alice. 'It isn't very likely there would be any mice on the horse's back.'

'Not very likely, perhaps,' said the Knight: 'but if they DO come, I don't choose to have them running all about.'

'You see,' he went on after a pause, 'It's as well to be provided for EVERYTHING. That's the reason the horse has all those anklets round his feet.'

'But what are they for?' Alice asked in a tone of great curiosity.

'To guard against the bites of sharks,' the Knight replied. 'It's an invention of my own. And now help me on. I'll go with you to the end of the wood—What's the dish for?'

'It's meant for plum-cake,' said Alice.

'We'd better take it with us,' the Knight said.

'It'll come in handy if we find any plum-cake. Help me to get it into this bag.'

This took a very long time to manage, though Alice held the bag open very carefully, because the Knight was so VERY awkward in putting in the dish: the first two or three times that he tried he fell in himself instead. 'It's rather a tight fit, you see,' he said, as they got it in a last; 'There are so many candlesticks in the bag.' And he hung it to the saddle, which was already loaded with bunches of carrots, and fire-irons, and many other things.

'I hope you've got your hair well fastened on?' he continued, as they set off.

'Only in the usual way,' Alice said, smiling.

'That's hardly enough,' he said, anxiously. 'You see the wind is so VERY strong here. It's as strong as soup.'

'Have you invented a plan for keeping the hair from being blown off?' Alice enquired.

'Not yet,' said the Knight. 'But I've got a plan for keeping it from FALLING off.'

'I should like to hear it, very much.'

'First you take an upright stick,' said the Knight. 'Then you make your hair creep up it, like a fruit-tree. Now the reason hair falls off is because it hangs DOWN—things never fall UPWARDS, you know. It's a plan of my own invention. You may try it if you like.'

It didn't sound a comfortable plan, Alice thought, and for a few minutes she walked on in silence, puzzling over the idea, and every now and then stopping to help the poor Knight, who certainly was NOT a good rider.

Whenever the horse stopped (which it did very often), he fell off in front; and whenever it went on again (which it generally did rather suddenly), he fell off behind. Otherwise he kept on pretty well, except that he had a habit of now and then falling off sideways; and as he generally did this on the side on which Alice was walking, she soon found that it was the best plan not to walk QUITE close to the horse.

'I'm afraid you've not had much practice in riding,' she ventured to say, as she was helping him up from his fifth tumble.

The Knight looked very much surprised, and a little offended at the remark. 'What makes you say that?' he asked, as he scrambled back into the saddle, keeping hold of Alice's hair with one hand, to save himself from falling over on the other side.

'Because people don't fall off quite so often, when they've had much practice.'

'I've had plenty of practice,' the Knight said very gravely: 'plenty of practice!'

Alice could think of nothing better to say than 'Indeed?' but she said it as heartily as she could. They went on a little way in silence after this, the Knight with his eyes shut, muttering to himself, and Alice watching anxiously for the next tumble.

'The great art of riding,' the Knight suddenly began in a loud voice, waving his right arm as he spoke, 'Is to keep—' Here the sentence ended as suddenly as it had begun, as the Knight fell heavily on the top of his head exactly in the path where Alice was walking. She was quite frightened this time, and said in an anxious tone, as she picked him up, 'I hope no bones are broken?'

'None to speak of,' the Knight said, as if he

didn't mind breaking two or three of them. 'The great art of riding, as I was saying, is—to keep your balance properly. Like this, you know—'

He let go the bridle, and stretched out both his arms to show Alice what he meant, and this time he fell flat on his back, right under the horse's feet.

'Plenty of practice!' he went on repeating, all the time that Alice was getting him on his feet again. 'Plenty of practice!'

'It's too ridiculous!' cried Alice, losing all her patience this time. 'You ought to have a wooden horse on wheels, that you ought!'

'Does that kind go smoothly?' the Knight asked in a tone of great interest, clasping his arms round the horse's neck as he spoke, just in time to save himself from tumbling off again.

'Much more smoothly than a live horse,' Alice said, with a little scream of laughter, in spite of all she could do to prevent it.

'I'll get one,' the Knight said thoughtfully to himself. 'One or two—several.'

There was a short silence after this, and then

the Knight went on again. 'I'm a great hand at inventing things. Now, I daresay you noticed, that last time you picked me up, that I was looking rather thoughtful?'

'You WERE a little grave,' said Alice.

'Well, just then I was inventing a new way of getting over a gate—would you like to hear it?'

'Very much indeed,' Alice said politely.

'I'll tell you how I came to think of it,' said the Knight. 'You see, I said to myself, "The only difficulty is with the feet: the HEAD is high enough already." Now, first I put my head on the top of the gate—then I stand on my head—then the feet are high enough, you see—then I'm over, you see.'

'Yes, I suppose you'd be over when that was done,' Alice said thoughtfully: 'but don't you think it would be rather hard?'

'I haven't tried it yet,' the Knight said, gravely: 'so I can't tell for certain—but I'm afraid it WOULD be a little hard.'

He looked so vexed at the idea, that Alice changed the subject hastily. 'What a curious helmet you've got!' she said cheerfully. 'Is that your invention too?'

The Knight looked down proudly at his helmet, which hung from the saddle. 'Yes,' he said, 'but I've invented a better one than that—like a sugar loaf. When I used to wear it, if I fell off the horse, it always touched the ground directly. So I had a VERY little way to fall, you see—But there WAS the danger of falling INTO it, to be sure. That happened to me once—and the worst of it was, before I could get out again, the other White Knight came and put it on. He thought it was his own helmet.'

The knight looked so solemn about it that Alice did not dare to laugh. 'I'm afraid you must have hurt him,' she said in a trembling voice, 'being on the top of his head.'

'I had to kick him, of course,' the Knight said, very seriously. 'And then he took the helmet off again—but it took hours and hours to get me out. I was as fast as—as lightning, you know.'

'But that's a different kind of fastness,' Alice objected.

The Knight shook his head. 'It was all kinds of

fastness with me, I can assure you!' he said. He raised his hands in some excitement as he said this, and instantly rolled out of the saddle, and fell headlong into a deep ditch.

Alice ran to the side of the ditch to look for him. She was rather startled by the fall, as for some time he had kept on very well, and she was afraid that he really WAS hurt this time. However, though she could see nothing but the soles of his feet, she was much relieved to hear that he was talking on in his usual tone. 'All kinds of fastness,' he repeated: 'but it was careless of him to put another man's helmet on—with the man in it, too.'

'How CAN you go on talking so quietly, head downwards?' Alice asked, as she dragged him out by the feet, and laid him in a heap on the bank.

The Knight looked surprised at the question. 'What does it matter where my body happens to be?' he said. 'My mind goes on working all the same. In fact, the more head downwards I am, the more I keep inventing new things.'

'Now the cleverest thing of the sort that I ever did,' he went on after a pause, 'was inventing a new pudding during the meat-course.'

'In time to have it cooked for the next course?' said Alice. 'Well, not the NEXT course,' the Knight said in a slow thoughtful tone: 'no, certainly not the next COURSE.'

'Then it would have to be the next day. I suppose you wouldn't have two pudding-courses in one dinner?'

'Well, not the NEXT day,' the Knight repeated as before: 'not the next DAY. In fact,' he went on, holding his head down, and his voice getting lower and lower, 'I don't believe that pudding ever WAS cooked! In fact, I don't believe that pudding ever WILL be cooked! And yet it was a very clever pudding to invent.'

'What did you mean it to be made of?' Alice asked, hoping to cheer him up, for the poor Knight seemed quite low-spirited about it.

'It began with blotting paper,' the Knight answered with a groan.

'That wouldn't be very nice, I'm afraid—'

'Not very nice ALONE,' he interrupted, quite eagerly: 'but you've no idea what a difference it makes mixing it with other things—such as gunpowder and sealing-wax. And here I must leave you.' They had just come to the end of the wood.

Alice could only look puzzled: she was thinking of the pudding.

'You are sad,' the Knight said in an anxious tone: 'let me sing you a song to comfort you.'

'Is it very long?' Alice asked, for she had heard a good deal of poetry that day.

'It's long,' said the Knight, 'but very, VERY beautiful. Everybody that hears me sing it—either it brings the TEARS into their eyes, or else—'

'Or else what?' said Alice, for the Knight had made a sudden pause.

'Or else it doesn't, you know. The name of the song is called "HADDOCKS' EYES."'

'Oh, that's the name of the song, is it?' Alice said, trying to feel interested.

'No, you don't understand,' the Knight said, looking a little vexed. 'That's what the name is CALLED. The name really IS "THE AGED AGED MAN."'

'Then I ought to have said "That's what the

SONG is called"?' Alice corrected herself.

'No, you oughtn't: that's quite another thing! The SONG is called "WAYS AND MEANS": but that's only what it's CALLED, you know!'

'Well, what IS the song, then?' said Alice, who was by this time completely bewildered.

'I was coming to that,' the Knight said. 'The song really IS "A-SITTING ON A GATE": and the tune's my own invention.'

So saying, he stopped his horse and let the reins fall on its neck: then, slowly beating time with one hand, and with a faint smile lighting up his gentle foolish face, as if he enjoyed the music of his song, he began.

Of all the strange things that Alice saw in her journey Through The Looking-Glass, this was the one that she always remembered most clearly. Years afterwards she could bring the whole scene back again, as if it had been only yesterday—the mild blue eyes and kindly smile of the Knight— the setting sun gleaming through his hair, and shining on his armour in a blaze of light that quite dazzled her—the horse quietly moving about, with

the reins hanging loose on his neck, cropping the
grass at her feet—and the black shadows of the
forest behind—all this she took in like a picture,
as, with one hand shading her eyes, she leant
against a tree, watching the strange pair, and listening, in a half dream, to the melancholy music
of the song.

'But the tune ISN'T his own invention,' she
said to herself: 'It's "I GIVE THEE ALL, I CAN NO
MORE."' She stood and listened very attentively,
but no tears came into her eyes.

> 'I'll tell thee everything I can;
> There's little to relate.
> I saw an aged aged man,
> A-sitting on a gate.
> "Who are you, aged man?"
> I said, "and how is it you live?"
> And his answer trickled through my head
> Like water through a sieve.
>
> He said "I look for butterflies
> That sleep among the wheat:

I make them into mutton-pies,
And sell them in the street.
I sell them unto men," he said,
"Who sail on stormy seas;
And that's the way I get my bread—

A trifle, if you please."

But I was thinking of a plan

To dye one's whiskers green,
And always use so large a fan
That they could not be seen.

So, having no reply to give
To what the old man said,

I cried, "Come, tell me how you live!"

And thumped him on the head.
His accents mild took up the tale:
He said "I go my ways,
And when I find a mountain-rill,
I set it in a blaze;
And thence they make a stuff they call
Rolands' Macassar Oil—
Yet twopence-halfpenny is all

They give me for my toil."

But I was thinking of a way

To feed oneself on batter,
And so go on from day to day
Getting a little fatter.
I shook him well from side to side,
Until his face was blue:

"Come, tell me how you live," I cried,

"And what it is you do!"


He said "I hunt for haddocks' eyes
Among the heather bright,
And work them into waistcoat-buttons
In the silent night.

And these I do not sell for gold
Or coin of silvery shine
But for a copper halfpenny,
And that will purchase nine.


"I sometimes dig for buttered rolls,
Or set limed twigs for crabs;
I sometimes search the grassy knolls
For wheels of Hansom-cabs.
And that's the way" (he gave a wink)

"By which I get my wealth—
And very gladly will I drink
Your Honour's noble health."

I heard him then, for I had just

Completed my design
To keep the Menai bridge from rust
By boiling it in wine.
I thanked him much for telling me

The way he got his wealth,
But chiefly for his wish that he
Might drink my noble health.


And now, if e'er by chance I put

My fingers into glue
Or madly squeeze a right-hand foot
Into a left-hand shoe,

Or if I drop upon my toe

A very heavy weight,
I weep, for it reminds me so,
Of that old man I used to know—


Whose look was mild, whose speech was slow,

Whose hair was whiter than the snow,
Whose face was very like a crow,
With eyes, like cinders, all aglow,
Who seemed distracted with his woe,
Who rocked his body to and fro,
And muttered mumblingly and low,
As if his mouth were full of dough,
Who snorted like a buffalo—
That summer evening, long ago,

A-sitting on a gate.'


As the Knight sang the last words of the ballad, he gathered up the reins, and turned his horse's head along the road by which they had come. 'You've only a few yards to go,' he said, 'down the hill and over that little brook, and then you'll be a Queen—But you'll stay and see me off first?' he added as Alice turned with an eager look in the direction to which he pointed. 'I shan't be long. You'll wait and wave your handkerchief when I get to that turn in the road? I think it'll encourage me, you see.'

'Of course I'll wait,' said Alice: 'and thank you

very much for coming so far—and for the song—I liked it very much.'

'I hope so,' the Knight said doubtfully: 'but you didn't cry so much as I thought you would.'

So they shook hands, and then the Knight rode slowly away into the forest. 'It won't take long to see him OFF, I expect,' Alice said to herself, as she stood watching him. 'There he goes! Right on his head as usual! However, he gets on again pretty easily—that comes of having so many things hung round the horse—' So she went on talking to herself, as she watched the horse walking leisurely along the road, and the Knight tumbling off, first on one side and then on the other. After the fourth or fifth tumble he reached the turn, and then she waved her handkerchief to him, and waited till he was out of sight.

'I hope it encouraged him,' she said, as she turned to run down the hill: 'and now for the last brook, and to be a Queen! How grand it sounds!' A very few steps brought her to the edge of the brook. 'The Eighth Square at last!' she cried as she bounded across,

\* \* \* \* \* \* \*

\* \* \* \* \* \*

\* \* \* \* \* \* \*

and threw herself down to rest on a lawn as soft as moss, with little flower-beds dotted about it here and there. 'Oh, how glad I am to get here! And what IS this on my head?' she exclaimed in a tone of dismay, as she put her hands up to something very heavy, and fitted tight all round her head.

'But how CAN it have got there without my knowing it?' she said to herself, as she lifted it off, and set it on her lap to make out what it could possibly be.

It was a golden crown.

# CHAPTER IX
# Queen Alice

'Well, this IS grand!' said Alice. 'I never expected I should be a Queen so soon—and I'll tell you what it is, your majesty,' she went on in a severe tone (she was always rather fond of scolding herself), 'It'll never do for you to be lolling about on the grass like that! Queens have to be dignified, you know!'

So she got up and walked about—rather stiffly just at first, as she was afraid that the crown might come off: but she comforted herself with the thought that there was nobody to see her, 'and if I really am a Queen,' she said as she sat down again, 'I shall be able to manage it quite well in time.'

Everything was happening so oddly that she didn't feel a bit surprised at finding the Red Queen and the White Queen sitting close to her, one on each side: she would have liked very much to ask them how they came there, but she feared it would not be quite civil. However, there would be no harm, she thought, in asking if the game was over. 'Please, would you tell me—' she began, looking timidly at the Red Queen.

'Speak when you're spoken to!' The Queen sharply interrupted her.

'But if everybody obeyed that rule,' said Alice, who was always ready for a little argument, 'and if you only spoke when you were spoken to, and the other person always waited for YOU to begin, you see nobody would ever say anything, so that—'

'Ridiculous!' cried the Queen. 'Why, don't you see, child—' here she broke off with a frown, and, after thinking for a minute, suddenly changed the subject of the conversation. 'What do you mean by "If you really are a Queen"? What right have you to call yourself so? You can't be a Queen, you know, till you've passed the proper examination. And the sooner we begin it, the better.'

'I only said "if"!' poor Alice pleaded in a piteous tone.

The two Queens looked at each other, and the Red Queen remarked, with a little shudder, 'She

SAYS she only said "if"—'

'But she said a great deal more than that!' the White Queen moaned, wringing her hands. 'Oh, ever so much more than that!'

'So you did, you know,' the Red Queen said to Alice. 'Always speak the truth—think before you speak—and write it down afterwards.'

'I'm sure I didn't mean—' Alice was beginning, but the Red Quee interrupted her impatiently.

'That's just what I complain of! You SHOULD have meant! What do you suppose is the use of child without any meaning? Even a joke should have some meaning—and a child's more important than a joke, I hope. You couldn't deny that, even if you tried with both hands.'

'I don't deny things with my HANDS,' Alice objected.

'Nobody said you did,' said the Red Queen. 'I said you couldn't if you tried.'

'She's in that state of mind,' said the White Queen, 'that she wants to deny SOMETHING-only she doesn't know what to deny!'

'A nasty, vicious temper,' the Red Queen remarked; and then there was an uncomfortable silence for a minute or two.

The Red Queen broke the silence by saying to the White Queen, 'I invite you to Alice's dinner-party this afternoon.'

The White Queen smiled feebly, and said 'And I invite YOU.'

'I didn't know I was to have a party at all,' said Alice; 'but if there is to be one, I think *I* ought to invite the guests.'

'We gave you the opportunity of doing it,' the Red Queen remarked: 'but I daresay you've not had many lessons in manners yet?'

'Manners are not taught in lessons,' said Alice. 'Lessons teach you to do sums, and things of that sort.'

'And you do Addition?' the White Queen asked. 'What's one and one and one and one and one and one and one and one and one?'

'I don't know,' said Alice. 'I lost count.'

'She can't do Addition,' the Red Queen interrupted. 'Can you do Subtraction? Take nine from eight.'

'Nine from eight I can't, you know,' Alice replied very readily: 'but—'

'She can't do Subtraction,' said the White Queen. 'Can you do Division? Divide a loaf by a knife—what's the answer to that?'

'I suppose—' Alice was beginning, but the Red Queen answered for her. 'Bread-and-butter, of course. Try another Subtraction sum. Take a bone from a dog: what remains?'

Alice considered. 'The bone wouldn't remain, of course, if I took it—and the dog wouldn't remain; it would come to bite me—and I'm sure I shouldn't remain!'

'Then you think nothing would remain?' said the Red Queen.

'I think that's the answer.'

'Wrong, as usual,' said the Red Queen: 'the dog's temper would remain.'

'But I don't see how—'

'Why, look here!' the Red Queen cried. 'The dog would lose its temper, wouldn't it?'

'Perhaps it would,' Alice replied cautiously.

'Then if the dog went away, its temper would

remain!' the Queen exclaimed triumphantly.

Alice said, as gravely as she could, 'They might go different ways.' But she couldn't help thinking to herself, 'What dreadful nonsense we ARE talking!'

'She can't do sums a BIT!' the Queens said together, with great emphasis.

'Can YOU do sums?' Alice said, turning suddenly on the White Queen, for she didn't like being found fault with so much.

The Queen gasped and shut her eyes. 'I can do Addition, if you give me time—but I can't do Subtraction, under ANY circumstances!'

'Of course you know your A B C?' said the Red Queen.

'To be sure I do.' said Alice.

'So do I,' the White Queen whispered: 'we'll often say it over together, dear. And I'll tell you a secret—I can read words of one letter! Isn't THAT grand! However, don't be discouraged. You'll come to it in time.'

Here the Red Queen began again. 'Can you answer useful questions?' she said. 'How is bread made?'

'I know THAT!' Alice cried eagerly. 'You take some flour—'

'Where do you pick the flower?' the White Queen asked. 'In a garden, or in the hedges?'

'Well, it isn't PICKED at all,' Alice explained: 'It's GROUND—'

'How many acres of ground?' said the White Queen. 'You mustn't leave out so many things.'

'Fan her head!' the Red Queen anxiously interrupted. 'She'll be feverish after so much thinking.' So they set to work and fanned her with bunches of leaves, till she had to beg them to leave off, it blew her hair about so.

'She's all right again now,' said the Red Queen. 'Do you know Languages? What's the French for fiddle-de-dee?'

'Fiddle-de-dee's not English,' Alice replied gravely.

'Who ever said it was?' said the Red Queen.

Alice thought she saw a way out of the difficulty this time. 'If you'll tell me what language "fiddle-de-dee" is, I'll tell you the French for it!'

she exclaimed triumphantly.

But the Red Queen drew herself up rather stiffly, and said 'Queens never make bargains.'

'I wish Queens never asked questions,' Alice thought to herself.

'Don't let us quarrel,' the White Queen said in an anxious tone. 'What is the cause of lightning?'

'The cause of lightning,' Alice said very decidedly, for she felt quite certain about this, 'Is the thunder—no, no!' she hastily corrected herself. 'I meant the other way.'

'It's too late to correct it,' said the Red Queen: 'when you've once said a thing, that fixes it, and you must take the consequences.'

'Which reminds me—' the White Queen said, looking down and nervously clasping and unclasping her hands, 'we had SUCH a thunderstorm last Tuesday—I mean one of the last set of Tuesdays, you know.'

Alice was puzzled. 'In OUR country,' she remarked, 'there's only one day at a time.'

The Red Queen said, 'That's a poor thin way of doing things. Now HERE, we mostly have days and nights two or three at a time, and sometimes in the winter we take as many as five nights together—for warmth, you know.'

'Are five nights warmer than one night, then?' Alice ventured to ask.

'Five times as warm, of course.'

'But they should be five times as COLD, by the same rule—'

'Just so!' cried the Red Queen. 'Five times as warm, AND five times as cold—just as I'm five times as rich as you are, AND five times as clever!'

Alice sighed and gave it up. 'It's exactly like a riddle with no answer!' she thought.

'Humpty Dumpty saw it too,' the White Queen went on in a low voice, more as if she were talking to herself. 'He came to the door with a corkscrew in his hand—'

'What did he want?' said the Red Queen.

'He said he WOULD come in,' the White Queen went on, 'because he was looking for a hippopotamus. Now, as it happened, there wasn't such a thing in the house, that morning.'

'Is there generally?' Alice asked in an astonished tone.

'Well, only on Thursdays,' said the Queen.

'I know what he came for,' said Alice: 'he wanted to punish the fish, because—'

Here the White Queen began again. 'It was SUCH a thunderstorm, you can't think!' ('She NEVER could, you know,' said the Red Queen.) 'And part of the roof came off, and ever so much thunder got in—and it went rolling round the room in great lumps—and knocking over the tables and things—till I was so frightened, I couldn't remember my own name!'

Alice thought to herself, 'I never should TRY to remember my name in the middle of an accident! Where would be the use of it?' but she did not say this aloud, for fear of hurting the poor Queen's feeling.

'Your Majesty must excuse her,' the Red Queen said to Alice, taking one of the White Queen's hands in her own, and gently stroking it: 'she means well, but she can't help saying foolish things, as a general rule.'

The White Queen looked timidly at Alice, who

felt she OUGHT to say something kind, but really couldn't think of anything at the moment.

'She never was really well brought up,' the Red Queen went on: 'but it's amazing how good-tempered she is! Pat her on the head, and see how pleased she'll be!' But this was more than Alice had courage to do.

'A little kindness—and putting her hair in papers—would do wonders with her—'

The White Queen gave a deep sigh, and laid her head on Alice's shoulder. 'I AM so sleepy?' she moaned.

'She's tired, poor thing!' said the Red Queen. 'Smooth her hair—lend her your nightcap—and sing her a soothing lullaby.'

'I haven't got a nightcap with me,' said Alice, as she tried to obey the first direction: 'and I don't know any soothing lullabies.'

'I must do it myself, then,' said the Red Queen, and she began:

'Hush-a-by lady, in Alice's lap!
Till the feast's ready, we've time for a nap:

When the feast's over, we'll go to the ball—
Red Queen, and White Queen, and Alice, and all!

'And now you know the words,' she added, as she put her head down on Alice's other shoulder, 'just sing it through to ME. I'm getting sleepy, too.' In another moment both Queens were fast asleep, and snoring loud.

'What AM I to do?' exclaimed Alice, looking about in great perplexity, as first one round head, and then the other, rolled down from her shoulder, and lay like a heavy lump in her lap. 'I don't think it EVER happened before, that any one had to take care of two Queens asleep at once! No, not in all the History of England—it couldn't, you know, because there never was more than one Queen at a time. Do wake up, you heavy things!' she went on in an impatient tone; but there was no answer but a gentle snoring.

The snoring got more distinct every minute, and sounded more like a tune: at last she could even make out the words, and she listened so eagerly that, when the two great heads vanished from her lap, she hardly missed them.

She was standing before an arched doorway over which were the words QUEEN ALICE in large letters, and on each side of the arch there was a bell-handle; one was marked 'Visitors' Bell,' and the other 'Servants' Bell.'

'I'll wait till the song's over,' thought Alice, 'and then I'll ring—the—WHICH bell must I ring?' she went on, very much puzzled by the names. 'I'm not a visitor, and I'm not a servant. There OUGHT to be one marked "Queen," you know—'

Just then the door opened a little way, and a creature with a long beak put its head out for a moment and said 'No admittance till the week after next!' and shut the door again with a bang.

Alice knocked and rang in vain for a long time, but at last, a very old Frog, who was sitting under a tree, got up and hobbled slowly towards her: he was dressed in bright yellow, and had enormous boots on.

'What is it, now?' the Frog said in a deep hoarse whisper.

Alice turned round, ready to find fault with anybody. 'Where's the servant whose business it is to answer the door?' she began angrily.

'Which door?' said the Frog.

Alice almost stamped with irritation at the slow drawl in which he spoke. 'THIS door, of course!'

The Frog looked at the door with his large dull eyes for a minute: then he went nearer and rubbed it with his thumb, as if he were trying whether the paint would come off; then he looked at Alice.

'To answer the door?' he said. 'What's it been asking of?' He was so hoarse that Alice could scarcely hear him.

'I don't know what you mean,' she said.

'I talks English, doesn't I?' the Frog went on. 'Or are you deaf? What did it ask you?'

'Nothing!' Alice said impatiently. 'I've been knocking at it!'

'Shouldn't do that—shouldn't do that—' the Frog muttered. 'Vexes it, you know.' Then he went up and gave the door a kick with one of his great feet. 'You let IT alone,' he panted out, as he hobbled back to his tree, 'and it'll let YOU alone, you know.'

At this moment the door was flung open, and a shrill voice was heard singing:

'To the Looking-Glass world it was Alice that said,
"I've a sceptre in hand, I've a crown on my head;
Let the Looking-Glass creatures, whatever they be,
Come and dine with the Red Queen, the White Queen, and me."'

And hundreds of voices joined in the chorus:

'Then fill up the glasses as quick as you can,
And sprinkle the table with buttons and bran:
Put cats in the coffee, and mice in the tea—
And welcome Queen Alice with thirty-times-three!'

Then followed a confused noise of cheering,

and Alice thought to herself, 'Thirty times three makes ninety. I wonder if any one's counting?' In a minute there was silence again, and the same shrill voice sang another verse;

"'O Looking-Glass creatures," quoth Alice,
"draw near!
'Tis an honour to see me, a favour to hear:
'Tis a privilege high to have dinner and tea
Along with the Red Queen, the White Queen, and me!'"

Then came the chorus again:—

'Then fill up the glasses with treacle and ink,
Or anything else that is pleasant to drink:
Mix sand with the cider, and wool with the wine—
And welcome Queen Alice with ninety-times-nine!'

'Ninety times nine!' Alice repeated in despair, 'Oh, that'll never be done! I'd better go in at once—' and there was a dead silence the moment she appeared.

Alice glanced nervously along the table, as she walked up the large hall, and noticed that there were about fifty guests, of all kinds: some were animals, some birds, and there were even a few flowers among them. 'I'm glad they've come without waiting to be asked,' she thought: 'I should never have known who were the right people to invite!'

There were three chairs at the head of the table; the Red and White Queens had already taken two of them, but the middle one was empty. Alice sat down in it, rather uncomfortable in the silence, and longing for some one to speak.

At last the Red Queen began. 'You've missed the soup and fish,' she said. 'Put on the joint!' And the waiters set a leg of mutton before Alice, who looked at it rather anxiously, as she had never had to carve a joint before.

'You look a little shy; let me introduce you to that leg of mutton,' said the Red Queen. 'Alice-Mutton; Mutton—Alice.' The leg of mutton got up in the dish and made a little bow to Alice; and Alice returned the bow, not knowing whether to be frightened or amused.

'May I give you a slice?' she said, taking up the knife and fork, and looking from one Queen to the other.

'Certainly not,' the Red Queen said, very decidedly: 'It isn't etiquette to cut any one you've been introduced to. Remove the joint!' And the waiters carried it off, and brought a large plum-pudding in its place.

'I won't be introduced to the pudding, please,' Alice said rather hastily, 'or we shall get no dinner at all. May I give you some?'

But the Red Queen looked sulky, and growled 'Pudding—Alice; Alice—Pudding. Remove the pudding!' and the waiters took it away so quickly that Alice couldn't return its bow.

However, she didn't see why the Red Queen should be the only one to give orders, so, as an experiment, she called out 'Waiter! Bring back the pudding!' and there it was again in a moment like a conjuring-trick. It was so large that she couldn't help feeling a LITTLE shy with it, as she had been with the mutton; however, she conquered her shyness by a great effort and cut a slice and handed it to the Red Queen.

'What impertinence!' said the Pudding. 'I wonder how you'd like it, if I were to cut a slice out of YOU, you creature!'

It spoke in a thick, suety sort of voice, and Alice hadn't a word to say in reply: she could only sit and look at it and gasp.

'Make a remark,' said the Red Queen: 'It's ridiculous to leave all the conversation to the pudding!'

'Do you know, I've had such a quantity of poetry repeated to me to-day,' Alice began, a little frightened at finding that, the moment she opened her lips, there was dead silence, and all eyes were fixed upon her; 'and it's a very curious thing, I think—every poem was about fishes in some way. Do you know why they're so fond of fishes, all about here?'

She spoke to the Red Queen, whose answer was a little wide of the mark. 'As to fishes,' she said, very slowly and solemnly, putting her mouth close to Alice's ear, 'her White Majesty knows a lovely riddle—all in poetry—all about fishes. Shall she repeat it?'

'Her Red Majesty's very kind to mention it,' the White Queen murmured into Alice's other ear, in a voice like the cooing of a pigeon. 'It would be SUCH a treat! May I?'

'Please do,' Alice said very politely.

The White Queen laughed with delight, and stroked Alice's cheek. Then she began:

'"First, the fish must be caught."
That is easy: a baby, I think, could have caught it.

"Next, the fish must be bought."
That is easy: a penny, I think, would have bought it.

"Now cook me the fish!"
That is easy, and will not take more than a minute.

"Let it lie in a dish!"
That is easy, because it already is in it.

"Bring it here! Let me sup!"

It is easy to set such a dish on the table.

"Take the dish-cover up!"

Ah, THAT is so hard that I fear I'm unable!

For it holds it like glue—
Holds the lid to the dish, while it lies in the middle:

Which is easiest to do,
Un-dish-cover the fish, or dishcover the riddle?'

'Take a minute to think about it, and then guess,' said the Red Queen. 'Meanwhile, we'll drink your health—Queen Alice's health!' she screamed at the top of her voice, and all the guests began drinking it directly, and very queerly they managed it: some of them put their glasses upon their heads like extinguishers, and drank all that trickled down their faces—others upset the decanters, and drank the wine as it ran off the edges of the table—and three of them (who looked like kangaroos) scrambled into the dish of roast mutton, and began eagerly lapping up the gravy, 'just like pigs in a trough!' thought Alice.

'You ought to return thanks in a neat speech,' the Red Queen said, frowning at Alice as she spoke.

'We must support you, you know,' the White Queen whispered, as Alice got up to do it, very obediently, but a little frightened.

'Thank you very much,' she whispered in reply, 'but I can do quite well without.'

'That wouldn't be at all the thing,' the Red Queen said very decidedly: so Alice tried to submit to it with a good grace.

('And they DID push so!' she said afterwards, when she was telling her sister the history of the feast. 'You would have thought they wanted to squeeze me flat!')

In fact it was rather difficult for her to keep in her place while she made her speech: the two Queens pushed her so, one on each side, that they nearly lifted her up into the air: 'I rise to return thanks—' Alice began: and she really DID rise as she spoke, several inches; but she got hold of the edge of the table, and managed to pull herself down again.

'Take care of yourself!' screamed the White Queen, seizing Alice's hair with both her hands. 'Something's going to happen!'

And then (as Alice afterwards described it) all sorts of things happened in a moment. The candles all grew up to the ceiling, looking something like a bed of rushes with fireworks at the top. As to the bottles, they each took a pair of plates, which they hastily fitted on as wings, and so, with forks for legs, went fluttering about in all directions: 'and very like birds they look,' Alice thought to herself, as well as she could in the dreadful confusion that was beginning.

At this moment she heard a hoarse laugh at her side, and turned to see what was the matter with the White Queen; but, instead of the Queen, there was the leg of mutton sitting in the chair. 'Here I am!' cried a voice from the soup tureen, and Alice turned again, just in time to see the Queen's broad good-natured face grinning at her for a moment over the edge of the tureen, before she disappeared into the soup.

There was not a moment to be lost. Already several of the guests were lying down in the dishes, and the soup ladle was walking up the table towards Alice's chair, and beckoning to her impatiently to get out of its way.

'I can't stand this any longer!' she cried as she jumped up and seized the table-cloth with both hands: one good pull, and plates, dishes, guests, and candles came crashing down together in a heap on the floor.

'And as for YOU,' she went on, turning fiercely upon the Red Queen, whom she considered as the cause of all the mischief—but the Queen was no longer at her side—she had suddenly dwindled down to the size of a little doll, and was now on the table, merrily running round and round after her own shawl, which was trailing behind her.

At any other time, Alice would have felt surprised at this, but she was far too much excited to be surprised at anything NOW. 'As for YOU,' she repeated, catching hold of the little creature in the very act of jumping over a bottle which had just

lighted upon the table, 'I'll shake you into a kitten,
흔들어서 작은 고양이로 만들다
that I will!'

# CHAPTER X
## Shaking

She took her off the table as she spoke, and shook her backwards and forwards with all her might.

The Red Queen made no resistance whatever; only her face grew very small, and her eyes got large and green: and still, as Alice went on shaking her, she kept on growing shorter—and fatter—and softer—and rounder—and—

## CHAPTER XI

## Waking

—and it really WAS a kitten, after all.
새끼고양이

# CHAPTER XII

## Which Dreamed it?

'Your majesty shouldn't purr so loud,' Alice said, rubbing her eyes, and addressing the kitten, respectfully, yet with some severity. 'You woke me out of oh! such a nice dream! And you've been along with me, Kitty—all through the Looking-Glass world. Did you know it, dear?'

It is a very inconvenient habit of kittens (Alice had once made the remark) that, whatever you say to them, they ALWAYS purr. 'If they would only purr for "yes" and mew for "no," or any rule of that sort,' she had said, 'so that one could keep up a conversation! But how CAN you talk with a person if they always say the same thing?'

On this occasion the kitten only purred: and it was impossible to guess whether it meant 'yes' or 'no.'

So Alice hunted among the chessmen on the table till she had found the Red Queen: then she went down on her knees on the hearth-rug, and put the kitten and the Queen to look at each other. 'Now, Kitty!' she cried, clapping her hands triumphantly. 'Confess that was what you turned into!'

('But it wouldn't look at it,' she said, when she was explaining the thing afterwards to her sister: 'It turned away its head, and pretended not to see it: but it looked a LITTLE ashamed of itself, so I think it MUST have been the Red Queen.')

'Sit up a little more stiffly, dear!' Alice cried with a merry laugh. 'And curtsey while you're thinking what to—what to purr. It saves time, remember!' And she caught it up and gave it one little kiss, 'just in honour of having been a Red Queen.'

'Snowdrop, my pet!' she went on, looking over her shoulder at the White Kitten, which was still patiently undergoing its toilet, 'when WILL Dinah have finished with your White Majesty, I wonder? That must be the reason you were so untidy in my dream—Dinah! do you know that you're scrubbing a White Queen? Really, it's most disrespectful of you!

'And what did DINAH turn to, I wonder?' she

prattled on, as she settled comfortably down, with one elbow in the rug, and her chin in her hand, to watch the kittens. 'Tell me, Dinah, did you turn to Humpty Dumpty? I THINK you did—however, you'd better not mention it to your friends just yet, for I'm not sure.

'By the way, Kitty, if only you'd been really with me in my dream, there was one thing you WOULD have enjoyed—I had such a quantity of poetry said to me, all about fishes! To-morrow morning you shall have a real treat. All the time you're eating your breakfast, I'll repeat "The Walrus and the Carpenter" to you; and then you can make believe it's oysters, dear!

'Now, Kitty, let's consider who it was that dreamed it all. This is a serious question, my dear, and you should NOT go on licking your paw like that—as if Dinah hadn't washed you this morning! You see, Kitty, it MUST have been either me or the Red King. He was part of my dream, of course—but then I was part of his dream, too! WAS it the Red King, Kitty? You were his wife, my dear, so you ought to know—Oh, Kitty, DO help to settle it! I'm sure your paw can wait!' But the provoking kitten only began on the other paw, and pretended it hadn't heard the question.

Which do YOU think it was?

——

A boat beneath a sunny sky,
Lingering onward dreamily
In an evening of July—

Children three that nestle near,
Eager eye and willing ear,
Pleased a simple tale to hear—

Long has paled that sunny sky:
Echoes fade and memories die.
Autumn frosts have slain July.

Still she haunts me, phantomwise,
Alice moving under skies
Never seen by waking eyes.

Children yet, the tale to hear,

Eager eye and willing ear,

Lovingly shall nestle near.

In a Wonderland they lie,
이상한 나라에 누워서
Dreaming as the days go by,
날이 저물도록 꿈꾸고
Dreaming as the summers die:
여름이 다 가도록 꿈꾸다

Ever drifting down the stream—
(물, 공기에) 떠가다, 표류[부유]하다
Lingering in the golden gleam—
환하다[반짝이다]
Life, what is it but a dream?
삶이란, 한낮 꿈이 아니던가?

# THE END

# 📖 나만의 리뷰 *and* 명문장